Jez Bond an

Jack and

Bloomsbury, Methuen Drama
An imprint of Bloomsbury Publishing Plc

B L O O M S B U R Y
LONDON · NEW DELHI · NEW YORK · SYDNEY

Bloomsbury Methuen Drama

An imprint of Bloomsbury Publishing Plc

50 Bedford Square	1385 Broadway
London	New York
WC1B 3DP	NY 10018
UK	USA

www.bloomsbury.com

**BLOOMSBURY, METHUEN DRAMA and the Diana
logo are trademarks of Bloomsbury Publishing Plc**

This playtext first published by Bloomsbury Methuen Drama 2015

Book © Jez Bond and Mark Cameron, 2015

Music & Lyrics © Jez Bond and Mark Cameron, 2015

British Library Cataloguing-in-Publication Data
A catalogue record for this book is available from the British Library.

ISBN: PB: 978-1-4742-4191-5
EPUB: 978-1-4742-4193-9
EPDF: 978-1-4742-4192-2

Library of Congress Cataloging-in-Publication Data
A catalog record for this title is available from the Library of Congress.

Typeset by Mark Heslington Ltd, Scarborough, North Yorkshire
Printed and bound in Great Britain

PARK THEATRE

Park Theatre is a theatre for London today. Our vision is to become a nationally and internationally recognised powerhouse of theatre.

★★★★★ *"A spanking new five-star neighbourhood theatre."* Independent

We opened in May 2013 and stand proudly at the heart of our diverse Finsbury Park community. With two theatres, a rehearsal and workshop space plus an all-day cafe bar, our mission is to be a welcoming and vibrant destination for all.

We choose plays based on how they make us feel: presenting classics through to new writing, musicals to experimental theatre all united by strong narrative drive and emotional content. In our first year we presented twenty-five plays including ten world premieres and two UK premieres, welcoming over one hundred and twenty seven thousand visitors through our doors.

Highlights included *Daytona*, with Maureen Lipman, which toured nationally and recently transferred to the West End, and *Yellow Face* which transferred to the National Theatre Shed.

"A first-rate new theatre in north London." Daily Telegraph

In our second year we're looking forward to growing our audience base, forging partnerships internationally and continuing to attract the best talent in the industry. Through a range of creative learning activities we're also working with all ages to nurture new audiences and develop the next generation of theatre practitioners.

To succeed in all of this, ongoing support is of paramount importance. As a charity, with no public subsidy, none of this is possible without the help of our Friends, trusts and foundations and corporate sponsors. To find out more about us, our artistic programme and how you can support Park Theatre, please go to **parktheatre.co.uk**

Jack and the Beanstalk

CAST

Dame	Michael Cahill
Jack	Omar Ibrahim
Grimm	Gloria Onitiri
Geoff	Killian Macardle
Grenthel	Paige Round

All other parts played by members of the cast

CREATIVE TEAM

Co-Writer & Director	Jez Bond
Co-Writer	Mark Cameron
Musical Director / Orchestrator	Dimitri Scarlato
Costume Designer	Josephine Sundt
Lighting Designer	Arnim Friess
Sound Designer	Chris Bartholomew
Set Designer	Jonny Dobson
Choreographer	Melli Bond
Fight Director	Claire Llewellyn of RC-ANNIE Ltd
Assistant Musical Director	Rebecca Chalmers
Assistant Directors	Sophie Gill
	Tamar Saphra
Casting Directors	Lucy Jenkins CDG and
	Sooki McShane CDG

PRODUCTION TEAM

Production Manager	Sarah Cowan
Company Stage Manager	Sophie Sierra
Assistant Stage Manager	Lisa Lewis
Costume Supervisor / Wardrobe Mistress	Jessica Bishop
Producer (for Park Theatre)	John-Jackson (JJ) Almond

CAST

Michael Cahill trained at Arts Educational Schools in London. Credits include: *Candide*, Menier Chocolate Factory. *The Selfish Giant*, directed by Clio Barnard. His TV appearances include: *Emmerdale*, *The Royal* (ITV); *Dalziel and Pascoe*, *Trail of Guilt*, *Operation Cobra* (BBC) and the *Les Miserables* movie for Barricade Productions. He has worked extensively as a principal across the UK and London's West End including: Enjolras in *Les Misérables*, the title role of *Martin Guerre* (Prince Edward Theatre); Rusty in *Starlight Express* (Apollo Theatre); *King* (Piccadilly Theatre); *Joseph and the Amazing Technicolor Dreamcoat* (London Palladium). *Bauhinia*, *Tipping the Velvet* (National Theatre Studio). *Closer Than Ever* (Landor Theatre). *A Month in the Country* (Salisbury Playhouse). *Stepping Out, Merlin and the Winter King* and *Company* (Derby Playhouse). *A Funny Thing Happened on the Way to the Forum* (Theatre Royal York); *Her Benny* (Liverpool Empire). *My Father's Son* (Sheffield Crucible). *Wuthering Heights* (Poland and the Netherlands). Squire Dither in *Mother Goose* (Bury St Edmonds). *Jacques Brel is Alive and Well* (Kings Head Theatre). Michael has played the Scarecrow in three productions of the *Wizard of Oz*, most recently at West Yorkshire Playhouse and Birmingham Rep where he also appeared in *Masterpieces*. For the innovative Bridewell Theatre London he appeared in Michael John La Chuisa's *Hello Again, La La La Chuisa, There's Always a Woman, The Road You Didn't Take* and Guy Burgess in *An Englishman Abroad*. As a director: *Love of a Good Woman* (Newbury Evolve Project), *Can't Stand Up for Falling Down* and assisted on the UK premier of *Songs for a New World*. He has directed innumerable concerts across the world including *Les Misérables* and *Miss Saigon*. He has recorded many BBC Radio 2 performances and was lucky enough to play a series of wonderful roles in thirteen complete musicals including Young Buddy in *Follies*; Henrik in *A Little Night Music*, Benny Southstreet in *Guys and Dolls*; Heavenly Friend in *Carousel*; Tranish in *Bitter Sweet* and Action in *West Side Story*.

Omar Ibrahim trained at the Guildford School of Acting. Theatre includes: *Warde Street* (Park Theatre); *News Revue* (Canal Cafe Theatre); *'Mohammed and I'* (Vault Festival); Shed (Rich Mix); *Acres* (New Diorama); *Theatre Uncut* (Young Vic, Drum Theatre and Barbican Theatre Plymouth); *Flat Sit* (Cockpit Theatre and Lost Theatre); *Hamlet* (UK and Ireland tour); *The Time of Your Life*

(Finborough Theatre); *Unseen* (V&A Museum); *Make Me a Martyr* (Finborough Theatre). Film includes: *Flat 32* (Comedy Pilot); *Missing Something* (Comedy Pilot Brother Brother); *Lying Down* (Fleeting Projects); *In The Pipeline* (Lonely Duck Productions).

Gloria Onitiri's theatre credits include: Anne in *Egusi Soup* (regional tour), Rachel Marron in *The Bodyguard* (Adelphi Theatre); *The Tempest* for Adrian Noble (Bath Theatre Royal); Charlotte in *Charlotte's Web* (Polka Theatre); Dionne in *Hair* (Festival Ljubljana); Sheila in *Takeaway* (Theatre Royal Stratford East); Arion in Cressida Brown's *Amphibians* (Bridewell); Nala in Disney's *The Lion King* (Lyceum); Simone in *Been So Long* (Young Vic); Aisha, Juliette and Violca in Dacia Maraini's *Hurried Steps* (New Shoes); understudy Mrs T, Girl Bear, Kate, Lucy and Gary Coleman in *Avenue Q* (Noel Coward); Bacchae in *The Bacchae* (National Theatre Scotland); Miss Sherman in *Fame* (Dutch tour); Morgan Le Fay in *Pendragon* (Northcott, Minack, Edinburgh Festival Theatre and Japan tour) and Sylvia in *The Dreaming* (Northcott and Linbury Studio, Royal Opera House). Film and television: Joy Okotume in *Doctors* (BBC); Knightriss in *Splatalot* (BBC, YTV, ABC); Jackie in *Resurrecting the Street Walker (Scala Films)*; Dotun in *The Window* (IWC); Marcia Jones in *Bad Girl* (Shed Productions) and Donna in *Grass* (BBC).

Killian Macardle trained at the Royal Central School of Speech and Drama. Television includes: Bill in *Glue* (Eleven Films for Channel 4). Theatre whilst training includes: Pathos in *The Twee Musketeers*; Roger in *Grease*; Chorus in *Cabaret*; Bobby in *Company*; Polonius in *Hamlet*; Morris in *Present Laughter*; Sytopka/Babushka/Gregoria in *Too Clever By Half*; Creon in *Antigone*; Edmond in *Edmond* and Feste in *Twelfth Night*.

Paige Round graduated from the Royal Central School of Speech and Drama earlier in the year. Her first professional job was playing Helena in *A Midsummer Night's Dream*, directed by Sasha McMurray. Other credits include: ensemble in *Pink Floyd -The Wall* workshop and The Messenger in *Antigone* at Belsize Park Festival.

Credits whilst training include: Rizzo in *Grease*; Gertrude in *Hamlet;* Amy in *Company*; Masha in *Three Sisters* and Madame Gloumova in *Too Clever By Half.*

Paige is delighted to be working at Park Theatre, and is looking forward to a fun festive season!

CREATIVES

Co-Writer / Director | Jez Bond

Jez graduated Hull University with a BA Honours in Drama and was awarded the Channel Four Theatre Director Bursary, under which he trained at Watford Palace Theatre. Jez is Artistic Director of Park Theatre which he founded.

As a director his credits include: *Sleeping Beauty* (which he co-wrote) and *Adult Supervision* (both for Park Theatre); *The Fame Game* (tour of Austria); *Sleeping Beauty* (Salisbury Playhouse); *Oliver!* (starring Rowan Atkinson, Oxford); *I Have Been Here Before* (Watford Palace Theatre); *The Twits* (tour of Switzerland); *Misconceptions* (Hong Kong Arts Centre); *Big Boys* (Croydon Warehouse); *Shot of Genius* (Leicester Square); *Canaries Sometimes Sing* (Kings Head and France) and *A Season in South Africa* (Old Vic). As a dramaturge he has worked with writers at Soho Theatre, Theatre Royal Stratford East, Royal Court and Young Vic.

Co-Writer | Mark Cameron

As an actor Mark's TV credits include: regular characters in *Coronation Street; Steel River Blues; Emmerdale; Doctors* plus guest roles in *Law and Order; Waterloo Road; Casualty; Holby City; EastEnders; The Roman Mysteries; Vincent; Mayo; The Royal; The Bill; Fifty Five Degrees North; Extreme Endurance* and *Brookside*. Film credits include: *Scar Tissue; The Boss* (2012 Reed Festival short film winner); *The Damned United; Casanova's Love Letters; Tomo* (Sundance Film Festival winner) and *The Other Side*. Theatre: *Mathematics of the Heart* (Theatre503 and winner of Brighton Fringe festival best play); *Sleeping Beauty* (Salisbury Playhouse); *The Game of Love and Chance* (national tour); *The Breakfast Soldiers* (Contact Theatre, Manchester); *The Taming of the Shrew* (Shakespeare in the Park); *Romeo and Juliet* (Cannizaro Park). Mark works extensively as a voice over artist for TV and radio.

As a writer Mark has worked with Jez Bond twice before, co-writing *Sleeping Beauty* (Park Theatre) as well as over one hundred sketches for *TooBigToPlay* (also with Mark Gillis). He is currently working on three sitcoms and a comedy-drama for television.

Musical Director / Orchestrator | Dimitri Scarlato

Dimitri was born and bred in Rome where he studied Composition, Piano and Conducting at the Conservatorio di Musica S. Sicilia. In 2004 he moved to London to attend an MMus in Composition at the Guildhall School of Music and Drama and he is currently completing his DMus in Composition at the Royal College of Music, which in 2010 selected him as an RCM Rising Star.

His music has been performed in several venues across Europe and Academia Filarmonica Romana (Italy) premiered his opera *Fadwa* (Teatro Olimpico, Rome) in May 2013. He is also heavily involved in film music; in 2007 he worked in the music pre-production of *Sweeney Todd*, directed by Tim Burton, and in 2009 he composed the music for *The City in the Sky*, which was selected for the 66th Venice Film Festival. In 2011 Dimitri was selected at *VOX3 – Composing for Voice* workshop at the Royal Opera House of London and at the Berlinale Talent Campus 2011 as a film composer. He is currently scoring the soundtrack for *Sparks and Embers*, a British independent film starring Kris Marshall. He has just finished coaching Michael Caine to be a conductor in the new film *Youth,* directed by Paolo Sorrentino. Dimitri lives and works in London.

www.dimitriscarlato.com

Costume Design | Josephine Sundt

Educated at Central Saint Martin's for a BA in Fashion Design Women's Wear, Josephine's graduate collection collaborated with dancers from the Royal Ballet Company, winning L'Oreal's Total Look Award, followed by a second collection which also on the Lancôme Modern Femininity Award.

Josephine has gone on to produce further contemporary designs for dancers of the Royal Ballet Company, English National Ballet, the Covent Garden Dance Company, as well as *Sleeping Beauty* for Park Theatre. Josephine compliments this with designs for private couture clients, drawing upon experience garnered as a design assistant for Claude Montana in Paris, as well as Roland Mouret, Tristan Webber and Julie Verhoeven in London.

Lighting Designer | Arnim Friess

Recent designs include: *Klook's Last Stand* (Park Theatre); *Alice in Wonderland* (Polka Theatre); *Ghosts in the Wall* (RSC); *Piaf* and

Gypsy (The Curve Leicester); *Leviathan* (Madrid); *Grandpa in My Pocket* (Nottingham Playhouse); *Wander* (Jockey Club Theatre Hong Kong); *The National Holocaust Memorial Day – The Rememberers* (Birmingham Rep); *A Roof of Light* (Coventry Cathedral's Blitz commemoration); *Lucky Seven* (Hampstead Theatre); *Looking for JJ* (Pilot Theatre, Unicorn); *One Night in November* (Belgrade Theatre Coventry); *The Suicide* and *An Inspector Calls* (Theatre Clwyd); *The White Album* (Nottingham Playhouse).

Sound Designer | Chris Bartholomew

Chris Bartholomew is a recent graduate of the Guildhall's Electronic Music Studios. Working as both a composer and sound designer for theatre, his recent credits include: sound design and music for *Light* by Theatre Ad Infinitum at the Edinburgh Fringe and transferring to the Barbican Pit in January; *The Curse of Elizabeth Faulkner* at the Charing Cross Theatre. As a music producer and technologist, Chris has been a long-time collaborator with Abandoman, overseeing the technical and musical aspects of their last two sell out Edinburgh shows which have then toured internationally.

Set Designer | Jonny Dobson

Jonny trained at Bishy School of Art and later under Sir Jodney Krant MBE at the prestigious Royal Landrian Touring Society. As designer, credits include: Tennesse William's *Giraffe on a Cold Sponge Ceiling*; *Waiting for Stobart*; *The Slight Tickling of Sister Barry*; Chekhov's *The Budgie* (in a new translation by Reginald Feld) and Arthur Miller's *Death of an Osteopath*. As associate, credits include: *Under Milk Johnson* (West End); *Who's Afraid of Quenteth Menenzies* (Number One Tour) and Pinter's *The Coming Betrayal of No Man's Birthday-Taker* (National Theatre).

Choreographer | Melli Bond

Melli graduated with a Bachelor Arts degree in Theatre and English Literature from the University of South Carolina and a Masters of Arts in Theatre Production from the University of Hull. She began studying acting and dance from the age of four. During her university years Melli was director of the Delaware Theatre Company Summer Arts Program (for young people), this is where she first began her work in creative learning. She has delivered workshops to children and adults for over twenty years in the

United States, Hong Kong and London. She began professional work as an actress in London in 2000. Melli co-founded Transmission, a workshop for professional actors, writers and directors.

Melli is the Creative Director and co-founder of Park Theatre. As head of creative learning she has developed the Program Script Accelerator to work with emerging artists, curates the exhibitions featured in the gallery space and has developed classes and projects for non-professionals of all ages.

As a choreographer her work includes: The Reduced Shakespeare Company's *The Bible: The Complete Word of God Abridged* (UK tour); *Sleeping Beauty* (Park Theatre); *Sleeping Beauty* (Salisbury Playhouse); *Oliver!* (starring Rowan Atkinson, Oxford); *The Fame Game* (Vienna's English Theatre); *The Master Forger* (The Tabard Theatre).

Fight Director | Claire Llewellyn of RC-ANNIE Ltd

Claire trained as an actor at Mountview College and it was here that her love of stage combat began. Claire trained as a stage combat teacher with the British Academy of Dramatic Combat (BADC) and is a current, serving member of its committee.

During her teacher training she was mentored by Rachel Bown-Williams and Ruth Cooper-Brown of RC-Annie with whom she is an associate teacher. Claire is the resident stage combat tutor at ALRA North.

Recent fight direction credits: *Macbeth*, *Romeo and Juliet*, *Oedipus at the Crossroads* (Tristan Bates Theatre). Fight assistant credits: *Red Velvet* (The Tricycle Theatre and Motion Pictures); *Arthur and Merlin* and *Howl* both to be released in 2015.

Assistant Musical Director | Rebecca Chalmers

Rebecca Chalmers is a versatile musician from Scotland. She graduated with distinction from the Guildhall School of Music and Drama with an MMus in flute performance in 2012. She is also an accomplished pianist and works as a musical director, accompanist, singing teacher, vocal animateur and workshop leader.

Rebecca has just returned to London after two years leading a music outreach project on the Caribbean island of Montserrat. As part of the project, which was initiated by Sir George Martin and the Montserrat Foundation UK, she founded and directed the National

Youth Choir of Montserrat and produced several musical productions.

She also holds a first class honours degree in Music and Spanish from Newcastle University where she was musical director of the university theatre society. She has worked as a musical director for Youth Music Theatre UK and is currently musical director of the new Dowsing Sound Collective in Hammersmith.

Assistant Director | Sophie Gill

After graduating from the University of Essex with a BA in Philosophy in 2006, Sophie spent several years working in IT projects for a range of financial institutions including Close Brothers Ltd and the Bank of England. She has recently left the world of banking to pursue her long-held dream of theatre directing. Previous credits as director: *No Exit* (Lakeside Theatre); *Hamlet* (City Lit, assistant); *STONEBREAKER* (City Lit Page to Stage) and *What's in the Coffee?* (Playground New Writing). Sophie is also creative business lead at Mental Fight Club, a Southwark-based charity that aims to promote good mental health through creativity and freedom of expression.

Assistant Director | Tamar Saphra

Tamar recently graduated with First Class Honours in English Literature and Theatre from the University of Sheffield where she was chair of the University Theatre Company. Her previous roles include general manager at The Finborough Theatre and she continues to review online for *A Younger Theatre*.

As a director/assistant director, her credits include: *No Fishing* and *Pillow Talk* (winners of Page To Stage, Tacchi Morris Arts Centre); *The Retold Ramayana* (assistant director, JayBird Live Literature); *Echoes Of Olympus* (A Festival of New Writing, SuTCo, Sheffield); *Build Me Up Buttercup* (assistant director, workshop dir. by Nikolai Foster); *A History of New Beginnings* (assistant director, Bare Project Theatre); *Hedda Gabler* (Sheffield University School of English), *Rope* (SuTCo, Sheffield).

Casting Directors | Lucy Jenkins CDG and Sooki McShane CDG

For Park Theatre: *Man to Man*; *The Man Who Shot Liberty Valance*; *Desdemona*; *Bomber's Moon*; *Sleeping Beauty*; *Adult Supervision* and *Casualties*.

Other theatre credits include: *All My Sons* and *Moon on a Rainbow Shawl* (Talawa/national tour); *To Kill a Mockingbird* (Regents Park and tour); *Our Country's Good* (Out Of Joint); *Much Ado About Nothing* (Royal Exchange Theatre); *War Horse* (UK tour/West End); *Solid Air* (Theatre Royal Plymouth); *Afraid of the Dark* (Charing Cross Theatre); *Tyne* (Live Theatre); *Chalet Lines* (Bush Theatre/Live Theatre); *Cooking with Elvis/Wet House* (Live Theatre/Soho); *Serpent's Tooth* (Almeida/Talawa); *The Glee Club* (Cast Theatre). For Nottingham Playhouse: *Time and the Conways*; *The Kite Runner*; *My Judy Garland Life*; *Richard III*; *The Ashes* and *Diary of a Football Nobody* and several productions for the Mercury Theatre, Colchester including *The Opinion Makers*; *The Butterfly Lion*; *The Good Person of Sichuan*; *The History Boys* and *The Hired Man*.

Television credits include: *Skins* (Company Pictures); *Wild at Heart* (Company Pictures); *The Bill* (Talkback Thames); *Samuel Johnson: The Dictionary Man* (October Films); *Family Affairs* (Talkback Thames).

Film credits include: *Awaiting* (Greenscreen); *Myrrdin* (Movieworks); *Containment* (Bright Cold Day Films); *Five-A-Side* (Emerald Films); *Entity* (Nexus DNA); *The Somnambulists* (No Bad Films); *Desi Boyz* (Desi Boyz Productions); *H10* (Dan Films).

PRODUCTION TEAM

Production Manager | Sarah Cowan

Through her career Sarah has production managed at many theatre in the UK including the Trafalgar Studios, Hampton Court and Theatre Royal Bath. She has also company stage managed with the RSC and Filter Theatre, Opera Holland Park and National Theatre Wales. In addition to theatrical work, she has event and festival experience in the fashion and music industries.

Company Stage Manager | Sophie Sierra

Sophie trained in Professional Stage Management at the Bristol Old Vic Theatre School.

Recent credits include: *The Backstage Tour* (Hoxton Hotel, Holborn); *The Nightmares of Carlos Fuentes* (Arcola Theatre); *Invisible Dot In The West End* (Duchess Theatre); *Fear and Loathing in Las Vegas* (Vaults Festival 2014).

Other credits include: *Dirty Dancing, The West End Story* (Piccadilly Theatre); *Laura Marling, Brazil, The Shawshank Redemption* and *Prometheus* (Secret Cinema); *Rapunzel* (Towngate Theatre); *Directors Cuts'* (Trafalgar Studios); *Future Cinema Takeover* (Wilderness Festival); *Events Whilst Guarding the Bofors Gun* (Finborough Theatre); *Dick Whittington and his Cat* (Theatre Royal Bury St Edmunds); *Mogadishu, Winterlong* (Royal Exchange Theatre, Manchester); *Bedlam* (Shakespeare's Globe).

Assistant Stage Manager | Lisa Lewis

Lisa Lewis studied Stage and Events Management at Royal Welsh College of Music and Drama and was involved in shows such as *Rent the Musical* and *The Magic Flute* as part of her studies.

Lisa has been working as a stage manager since finishing her masters in shows such as Oxford Shakespeare company's *As You Like It*; National Theatre Wales Team Projects; Aberystwyth Arts Centre's *Fame The Musical*; Louche Theatre's production's of *A Portrait of Dylan Thomas, A Child's Christmas in Wales* and *Lilies on the Land*, and was part of the stage management team in the Assembly Rooms in Edinburgh for the Fringe.

Lisa has just finished a work placement at the Royal Opera House working on *Idomeneo* and *Scala Di Seta*. She is looking forward to working on *Jack and the Beanstalk* at Park Theatre and hopes to keep up with all the Tupperware needs of the show.

Costume Supervisor / Wardrobe Mistress | Jessica Bishop

Jessica has recently graduated from the Royal Central School of Speech and Drama with a BA(Hons) in Costume Construction.

Alongside costume making she is also interested in costume breakdown and dyeing and is a casual worker at the Royal Opera House and has just finished working on the current season's operas and ballets. In her final year at university she worked with the Blue Sky Actors designing, making and supervising the costumes for their pantomimes. Last year, Jess worked alongside Kathy Burke at the Tricycle Theatre on *Once A Catholic* as assistant costume supervisor. She also designed and supervised the *No Barriers With Barriers* bowling show at Rowan's bowling alley earlier this year.

Jack and the Beanstalk

DRAMATIS PERSONAE

This musical can be performed by a cast of up to ten actors – plus, if desired, a chorus.

Below are the roles, with suggested doubling, for the minimum cast size of five.

Principals

Jack *[& Opening Scene* **Fencer/Hamlet***]*
Tupperware Tina, *Jack's mother* – **The Dame** *[&* **Claudius***]*
Geoff, *the smallest giant in the world [& Opening Scene* **Fencer/ Laertes/Gravedigger***]*
Grenthel, *his best friend [&* **Ophelia***]*
Ms Grimm, *Grenthel's mother [&* **Gertrude***]*

Suggested Doubling

The Shepherds Gonzalez:
Shepherd Dave – Jack
Shepherd Boutros – Tupperware Tina
Shepherd Kofi – Geoff
Shepherd Gary – Grenthel
Shepherd Ban Ki – Ms Grimm

Other:
Audience Member One – Geoff
Giant One – Jack
Giant Two – Tupperware Tina
Daisy, the Cow – Geoff
Audience Member Two – Grenthel
Audience Member Three – Grimm
Inspector – Ms Grimm
Giant Messenger – Jack
Bishy McGwendez – Grenthel
Umpire – Geoff
Narrator – divided up amongst all the actors
Actor, Stage Manager and Assistant Stage Manager lines to be given out as appropriate

NB: Audience Members four and five are genuine audience members

Pre-Recorded Voice-Overs (or live)
Commentator One
Commentator Two
Announcer

SONGS
SONG 1: FEE FI FO FUM (Act1, Sc1) - All
SONG 2: WE ARE THE SHEPHERDS* (Act1, Sc4) - All
SONG 3: IF I WERE* (Act1, Sc5) - Daisy the Cow
SONG 4: I'LL ALWAYS FIND YOU* (Act1, Sc6) - Grenthel
SONG 5: MY PLAN (Act1, Sc8) – Grimm
SONG 6: JUST CALL OUT OUR NAME (Act2, Sc1) - All
SONG 7: MY BOY (Ac2, Sc2) - Dame
SONG 8: CARA MISON (Act2, Sc3) – All
SONG 9: FEE FI FO FUM – REPRISE (Act2, Sc6) – All
SONG 10: SHEPHERD MEDLEY – REPRISE* (Act2, Epilogue) – All

Music & Lyrics by Jez Bond

*Music & Lyrics by Jez Bond & Mark Cameron

Footnotes by Mark Cameron

HISTIOGRAPHY[1]
Welcome fair reader to the wonderful world of Waa. Last year's *Sleeping Beauty* was the first instalment of *The Chronicles of Waa*. After much deliberation this year's *Jack and the Beanstalk* shall now be ever known as the second instalment of *The Chronicles of Waa*. Please take care not to confuse our *Jack and the Beanstalk*, with *Jackie and her Bishops*, *Janice and her Badgers* or Leopold Gonsom's classic *Julie and her Unmentionables*.

A NOTE ON PRONUNCIATION
The language of Waa is not for the faint-hearted. For those of a timid disposition Gregor Sembanni's peerless *Beginner's Guide to Gestures in Haberdashery* will have proven essential in navigating the mellifluous tones of the Pilipostian and

---

[1] See also hysterectomy, histamine, anti-histamine and Uncle Michael Heseltine.

Babuüsian dialects in last year's *Sleeping Beauty*. This year, however, the honeyed hues of Nowen are to be mastered. They are an entirely different kettle of bibbles. These bibbles mean business: bibble business. Easier on the nose they may be, but caution: all dialects from the region of Nowen require the appropriate footwear. As with all Waaian diphthongs they may appear soft under foot and often unnecessarily melodramatic in tone. The speaker should be encouraged to exaggerate the vowels and consonants as best he/she can (and may indeed form his or her decisions based on the few surviving manuscripts of the time – see Gwethton Pod's *Really Really Early Stuff Written In Waa* and the sequel *Not Quite As Early As The Really Really Early Stuff But Still Pretty Early Stuff Written In Waa*).

LOCATIONS
A State Room in Elsinore
Up in the Clouds
Deep in the Gazoobian Mountains
Jack's Farmhouse in Nowen
The Market Place in Nowen
The Woods near the Border
The Top of the Beanstalk

PRE-SHOW ANNOUNCEMENT (V/O)
Ladies and Gentlemen welcome to Park Theatre. Before the show begins, may we kindly ask you to switch off your mobile phones. Thank you and enjoy our production of Hamlet.

Act One

A State Room in Elsinore

Claudius, *King of Denmark*, **Gertrude** *the Queen and* **Polonius**
*watch a ceremonial rapier match. The match ends and the King and
his train applaud.*

Claudius   Though yet of Hamlet our dear brother's death
  The memory be green, and that to us befitted
  To bear our hearts in grief, and our whole kingdom
  To be contracted in one brow of woe
  Therefore our sometime sister, now our Queen
  The imperial jointress to this warlike state
  Have we as 'twere with a defeated joy
  With an auspicious and a drooping eye taken to wife

Hamlet *enters, dressed in black.*

Claudius   But now my cousin Hamlet and my son . . .

Hamlet   A little more than kin and less than kind.

Claudius   How is it that the clouds still hang on you?

Hamlet   Not so my lord, I am too much in the sun.

Gertrude   Good Hamlet cast thy nighted colour off
  And let thine eye look like a friend on the Dane
  Thou knowest 'tis common
  All that lives must die.

Claudius   'Tis sweet and commendable in your nature
Hamlet
  To give these mourning duties to your father
  But you must know your father lost a father
  That father lost, lost his.

Gertrude   Let not thy mother lose her prayers, Hamlet
  I pray thee stay with us, go not to Wittenberg.

Hamlet   I shall in all my best obey you, madam.

Gertrude *and* **Claudius** *exit.*

Hamlet O that this too too solid fresh would melt . . .

A phone rings in the auditorium . . .

Hamlet Thaw, and resolve itself into a dew
  Or that the Everlasting had not fixed

Audience Member One *answers his phone.*

Audience Member One Hello?

Hamlet His canon 'gainst self-slaughter! O God, God!

Audience Member One (*whispering on phone*) No, no
it's started.

Hamlet That it should come to this.

Audience Member One I don't know, it's a bit weird,
they're speaking Shakespeare or something.

Hamlet But two months dead . . .

Audience Member One (*still on phone*) I think I've got the
wrong the play.

Hamlet (*stumbling*) But two months dead . . .

Audience Member One (*getting up – to* **Hamlet**) Excuse me,
excuse me? (**Hamlet** *does his best to ignore him and moves away.*)
Alright, be like that.

Hamlet (*annoyed and distracted*) O that this . . .

Audience Member One *now crosses the stage in order to exit
the auditorium.*

Hamlet (*out of character*) What are you doing?

Audience Member One Leaving, that's what I'm doing.

Hamlet But this is The Tragedy of Hamlet, Prince of
Denmark! So if you don't mind . . . (*With a 'Shakespearean'
voice.*) Oh that this . . .

Audience Member One I do mind actually. I've got a ticket
for Jack and the Beanstalk!

Hamlet (*out of character*)   Jack and the Beanstalk?

Audience Member One (*exiting*)   Yeah.

Claudius (*out of character, entering*)   What's going on?

Gertrude (*out of character, entering half changed*)   Why've we stopped?

Hamlet (*out of character*)   It's nothing, really. Everything's fine. As you were everyone.

Claudius (*out of character*)   I'm sure I heard someone say they were here for Jack and the Beanstalk.

Hamlet *tries to hush them.*

Ophelia (*out of character, entering, hair in curlers*)   What's happening?

All (*to different members of the audience*)   Have you got tickets for Jack and the Beanstalk too?

The audience respond.

Claudius (*out of character*)   Good lord, we're doing the wrong play!

Hamlet (*out of character*)   But . . . but . . . we've started Hamlet now so we should crack on.

Ophelia (*out of character*)   That's not very fair. I think we should ask them. Which play do you *want* to see? Jack and the Beanstalk or Hamlet?

The audience respond.

Claudius (*out of character*)   Right, company, Jack and the Beanstalk it is!

Gertrude (*out of character*)   We haven't finished rehearsing it, Michael. (*Or real name of actor.*) Last time you went on underprepared you ended up in A and E with a cucumber . . .

Hamlet (*out of character*) . . . but I'm (the first British Asian)[2] Hamlet, this is the biggest opportunity of my career.

Laertes (*out of character*) And I was really looking forward to finally doing the gravedigger scene. My agent's in as well!

Ophelia (*out of character*) I think we should do Jack and the Beanstalk. Sorry, guys, Ophelia dies before the interval.

As general chaos ensues, the actors rush towards the actor playing **Claudius**. *The dialogue following overlaps, becoming all too confusing for him.*

Gertrude (*out of character*) Michael, (*Or real name of actor,*) we haven't even got props let alone the set. So I was thinking in the first scene whether I could just . . . .

Laertes (*out of character*) At least let me do the gravedigger scene. Please, Michael? (*Or real name of actor.*) If I could just get the gravedigger scene in there . . . .

Hamlet (*out of character*) If he's doing the gravedigger scene, I'm definitely gonna do my main speech from Hamlet . . .

Claudius (*out of character*) Enough! Please! Just do the best you can. We're professional actors after all! (*To the audience.*) Perhaps everyone can help? You'll help us, won't you? We're a bit short of a few essential items you see.

Laertes (*out of character*) Understatement!

Claudius (*out of character*) Thank you, Killian. (*Or real name of actor.*) But with your help, all will be well! Are we ready?

Like you, we believe that long stage directions are boring and should be avoided whenever possible. However, please read this next section otherwise the rest of the play won't make any sense.

The actors playing **Ophelia** *and* **Claudius** (*those most excited about doing Jack and the Beanstalk*) *talk to the audience, collecting costumes and props that they can use for their characters. The* **Dame**

---

[2] This was inserted to suit the actor in the original production.

asks someone in the front row to help do his makeup. A number of the
actors recruit audience members to draw pictures of some of the main
set locations on large white boards with coloured pens – these will
then be used during the performance. At one point the actor playing
Claudius *shouts: 'One minute to showtime!' The stage management*
run around preparing, the skull of Yorrick gets passed to an
audience member who is told to look after it and at one point an
actor rushes across the stage in just a pink pair of underpants.
Hamlet *is distraught, his big chance has gone.* **Laertes** *less so as he*
will still get to do his gravedigger bit. He advises **Hamlet** *to be more*
pushy. It's a frantic mess with people shouting out suggestions of how
they are going to double up and whom they are going to play in each
scene. In the middle of all this someone comes in rolling a large
costume rail, shouting 'costumes'. One of the actors comes on and sets
a stool and microphone at the side of the stage (for the narrated
sections).

Finally . . . the stage is clear.

Prologue

Up in the Clouds

An ethereal 'Ah-Ah-Ah-Ah' resounds. A figure with a white beard,
dressed in a mariachi outfit appears through the smoke . . .

Shepherd Kofi (*coughing from the excess smoke*)   Oh hello,
boys and girls! I'm here to tell you a story about the magical
land of Waa.[3] Some of you may have visited Waa before.
You've practiced the curious gestures of Pilipots,[4] tasted the
culinary delicacies of Babuüs[5] and even learnt some of the
language. Om-ba se-lay pa-du: the cat sat on the mat. But
our story today takes place in two places you've not yet

---

[3] A beautiful and fertile land stretching from the notorious Gazoobian mountains in
the East to the land locked Port of Quell Sang Fran in the middle of the Gazoobian
mountains.
[4] See *Sleeping Beauty*, Bond & Cameron, Methuen, First Edition 2013 for accompanying
gesture.
[5] See *Sleeping Beauty*, Bond & Cameron, Methuen, First Edition 2013.

visited. The treacherous mountains of Gazoob[6] and the luscious, green fields of Nowen.[7] Ooh I'm so sorry, I haven't introduced myself. Some people call us wizards, some people call us fairies, some people call us angels, some call us oracles – but generally, people just call us The Shepherds Gonzalez. (*An ethereal 'Ah-Ah-Ah-Ah'*) How about every time someone says 'The Shepherds Gonzalez' you go (*Sings.*) 'Ah-Ah-Ah-Ah'? Is that okay? Shall we try? Fantastic!

Shepherd Kofi *teaches the audience the response.*

During the next section the respective actors come on and off stage doing a dumb show of the narration.

Once upon a time, in the land of Waa lived a boy called Jack, his mother Tina and their precious cow Daisy. They lived a happy life, tilling the land (*The actors act this out.*) and playing with their balls. (*The actors juggle and throw balls.*) This was Nowen, a peaceful land and the spiritual home of Tupperware. But just three klenkths[8] away, deep in the mountains of Gazoob the evil Ms Grimm ran a workhouse for giants. Every day she forced these gentle giants to pick and pack the beans that grew there. All part of her wicked plan to take the over the world! The only ray of hope was the secret love between her delightful daughter Grenthel, and the noble Geoff, the smallest giant in the world, played by the beautiful and wonderfully subtle actor Killian Macardle . . . (*Or real name of actor.*)

Claudius (*out of character*)   . . . stick to the script, Killian! (*Or real name of actor.*)

Shepherd Kofi   Sorry, Michael! (*Or real name of actor.*) (*Resumes.*) Bye for now – there are a few of my kind and you will meet us again, later in the story . . .

---

[6] Similar and very different from the word 'randolph'. Mispronunciation can cause rashes on your Babboosays.

[7] A geographical anomaly. It only appears on non-foldable maps. The spiritual home of the towel.

[8] Officially the distance between an average sized thought and an un-averaged sized tonsil. Unofficially the distance between two badgers who are getting on 'very well'.

Scene One

Deep in the Gazoobian Mountains

One of the actors sits on a chair to speak. This becomes the 'narrator's chair' and whichever actor narrates generally assumes this position. A microphone may also be used.

Narrator   Grimm's Giant Workhouse, deep in the Gazoobian mountains.

SONG ONE: FEE FI FO FUM

[Various]   Here in the mountains
  Behind the iron gates
  There lies a workhouse
  For gentle giants
  Nobody loves us
  Inside this workhouse
  Nobody ever did . . .

Ms Grimm *enters with* **Grenthel**. **Grimm** *wears a homemade mechanical hair straightener with flashing lights.*

Grimm   Get to it, you snivelling wretches!

The song ups tempo and the orphan giants sing with forced gusto.

[All]   Up where the clouds lie
  Along the hillside
  Here where the sun shines on the crops all day
  We climb and gather
  Working together
  And so we sing this
  As we work away

  And yes we say [x3]
  Ms Grimm she is the very best by far
  Hi-di-hey-di-ah Hey ah Hey ah
  Fee Fi Fee Fi Fo Fum – Fee Fi Fo Fum

Grimm (*removing the hair straightener, her hair pops into a frizzy mop*)   Hmm, this new hair straightener needs work. (*Looking* *into it.*) Ah hah! I'll reset the dobby[9] and tighten up the squelding belt![10]

[All] We toil the land and
  We lend a hand and
  We work together as a giant team

[Giant One] I pick the finest

[Giant Two] I wash and dry best

[Geoff] I sort and sample

[All] THEN we pack the beans

  Do what we do best
  We never need rest
  And our reward is our economy
  Exporting beans as
  Our country needs us
  It's as easy as one, two, three

  And yes we say [x3]
  Ms Grimm she is the very best by far
  Hi-di-hey-di-ah Hey ah Hey ah
  Fee Fi Fee Fi Fo Fum – Fee Fi Fo Fum

Grimm You're here because you're trash. You're the rubbish giants, the unpopular, the unskilled, the unloved and quite frankly the un-loveable. But luckily you have me! Me to give you a chance to improve yourself, to make something better of your life. (*Grumbles from the giants.*) You ungrateful little goosbabas![11] Add ten more crates to your quota for the day.

Giant One But, Miss!

Grimm Eleven crates.

Giant Two But . . .

---

[9] A transitive verb of questionable use. May contain nuts.
[10] A standard hole-less, buckle-less trouser belt but with less manners.
[11] A grumpy land-based seahorse with wings but without the foresight, or Bruce Forsyth, to use them.

Grimm   Twelve crates.

All Giants   What?/No!/Not fair!

Grimm   Unless you want to go through the Door of Doom!

The Giants *fall silent.*

Grenthel   Mother!

Grimm   One has to be strong, Grenthel, or they'll never learn. (*Quietly.*) And don't ever question me in front of these disgusting giants again.

Grenthel   Being strong is one thing but being unnecessarily cruel is another.

Grimm   Maybe one day I'll tell you what these horrible creatures did to our family. Then you'll understand. (*We hear a sound effect 'Sister, sister'.*) Now fetch my latest invention. I'm in desperate need of relief.

Grenthel *passes her a large mechanical massaging backpack with a hand control, which* **Grimm** *wears. She turns it on and starts to roll her shoulders in pleasure.*

Grimm   Ooh yes, my Tupperware massaging kit. Mmm. Tupperware: pliable yet strong, durable yet stylistic, contemporary yet timeless. Ooh Tupperware.

Grimm *gets lost in this and is ignorant of the goings on with the workers for the next section.*

[**Giant One**]   But when the night falls
We're locked in darkness
Try to be brave with shadows everywhere

[**Giant Two**]   With every beating
All joy is fleeting
Dreaming of a different life

[**Geoff**]   Within this cruelty
Lives truest beauty
A girl I love who's always fair and true

[Grenthel]   Secret relations
   It takes some patience

[Both]   But when I'm with her/him I'm no longer blue

Grimm (*sensing a drop of energy in the workers*)   Enough dawdling!

One of them drops a crate.

Grimm   Who did that?

A moment, all terrified and nobody wanting to admit responsibility.

Geoff (*taking the blame for his friend*)   It was me.

Grimm   No food for you tonight.

Geoff   You call that food?

The Giants *snigger.*

Grimm   We have a joker do we? (*Pointing at* **Geoff**.) Let's see how funny you find it through the Door of Doom. Now!

The Giants *gasp.*

Grenthel (*going to stop her*)   No Mother . . .

Grimm   What?!

Grenthel (*correcting herself*)   No mother, let *me* punish him. I need to practice disciplining these worthless giants, like you said.

Grimm   Hmm . . . very well, Grenthel . . . (*Passing her whip.*) Show me! Three lashes. Actually, no – whipping is far too good for them. Make . . . the silent sound!

The Giants *recoil in horror.*

Grenthel   The silent sound? I really don't think that's necess . . .

Grimm   . . . fine then, the Door of Doom it is.

Grenthel   Okay, okay, I'll do it.

The Giants *are terrified.* **Grenthel** *begins to make the silent sound, contorting her face and pointing in her ears causing* **The Giants** *to writhe in agony. After a few moments she stops.*

Grimm   Maybe you will amount to something before your wedding day, after all. Now get these crates to the packing room. (*To* **Geoff.**) *You're* safe – this time!

She exits.

Grenthel   Geoff. I'm so sorry. I had to. No one's ever returned from beyond the Door of Doom.

Geoff   . . . then you saved my life.

Grenthel   But we can't risk staying here any longer. We have to escape tonight!

Geoff   But –

Grenthel   We're out of time. In case you've forgotten, mother's forcing me to marry the Prince of Senpebs[12] next week! She'll inherit all the quellb[13] in the Senpebian mines and become the most powerful woman in all of Gazoob. Then we'll all be doomed!

Geoff   But with your mother's crazy booby traps everywhere there's no way out!

Grenthel   There is. An old access hatch. I've seen it on the blueprints for the building. I'll steal them tonight.

Geoff   How?

Grenthel   Mum's off for her annual nose trim, she'll be ages.

Grimm *creeps back in, but* **Grenthel** *notices and immediately assumes her best 'horrible' voice.*

Grenthel   Return to your work, you useless giant!

---

[12] A vast village of minute proportions available in a variety of flavours.
[13] 'Dark matter' with a light fluffy centre.

Grimm   Better, Grenthel, better. Strong women have always been the backbone of Gazoobian life. A fine royal family we shall make. A fine royal family indeed!

Scene Two

Jack's Farmhouse in Nowen

Narrator   Three klenths away, as the Juju bird[14] flies, we're at Jack's farmhouse in Nowen.

As he continues to narrate an actor starts to act out the directions.

Narrator   In the distance, village folk work the fields, some harvest fruit from the trees, chickens cluck, a dog scratches its ear, the other ear, then rolls about on the floor and relieves itself against a tree.

The **Actor** *gestures to the* **Narrator***; 'really?!'*

Narrator   Yep, that's what it says here!

The **Actor** *looks to the actor who played* **Claudius***.*

Actor   Michael? (*Or real name of actor.*)

Claudius (*out of character*)   If it's in the script!

The **Actor** *does it.*

Narrator (*continuing*)   Jack and his mother Tina, enter with their cow, Daisy. (*They do so.*) They were happy.

Jack/Dame/Daisy   Yeah!

Narrator   And poor.

Jack/Daisy   Oh?!

Dame (*out of character*)   That's okay. Just because you're poor doesn't mean you're not happy.

---

[14] A mammal that often believes it's Hillary Clinton and will never forget to send a card on your birthday.

Stage Manager (*offstage*)   It's true. Money can't buy happiness. In fact (*Walking on and addressing the audience.*) many of the wealthiest people throughout history weren't happy.

Daisy (*out of character*)   Like who?

Stage Manager   Eddie Stobart.[15]

Jack (*out of character*)   He was unhappy?

Stage Manager   Oh, I don't know. I've just always wanted to stand on stage and say the words 'Eddie Stobart'.

Daisy (*out of character*)   Great. Are we done?

Stage Manager   Sorry, carry on.

Exits.

Narrator   They were happy and poor.

Jack/Dame/Daisy   Yeah!

All, apart from **Narrator**, *exit.*

Narrator   Today was the start of the Nowenthian annual festival, which, as always began with a free Tupperware evaluation. Oh yes!

Jack   Welcome to Nowen, the spiritual home of Tupperware. Who loves Tupperware? (*Audience don't react.*) Ah, a few of you are obviously unfamiliar with the appropriate response there. You see in Nowen when anyone asks 'who loves Tupperware' it's customary to reply 'we do!' Shall we give that a go?

Jack *interacts with the audience.* **Daisy** *thoroughly enjoys herself and interacts with audience too. Shaking hands, high fives etc. She also reacts to what* **Jack** *says throughout his speech and pleads with the audience to keep the promise.*

---

[15] Not to be confused with Eddie Stobart Logistics Ltd, the large British multimodal logistics company with interests in road haulage, rail freight, deep sea and inland waterway transport systems and deep sea port, inland port and rail-connected storage facilities, along with transport, handling and warehousing facilities through operations in the United Kingdom, Ireland and Belgium.

Jack   Amazing. I've just realised that some of you might not know the language here either. So why don't we take a quick look at the alphabet of Nowen, it's very easy to learn. Daisy, if you would.

Daisy *rushes off stage and comes back with what looks like a children's alphabet chart. He looks down at what he's wearing and shakes his head at the actor playing* **Jack**.

Daisy (*out of character*)   Three years at drama school!

Jack (*out of character*, to **Daisy**)   You're alright, I'm supposed to be Hamlet!

The alphabet chart is entitled 'The Alphabet of Nowen' and contains sixteen shapes and sounds:

A B C D E F Gé *H* Io J\ Kk ^ Lx+ : M(g) N-sh] 'O)_ P%/ti

Jack *proceeds to teach them the sounds and the silly gestures that accompany each of the letters. All the while* **Daisy** *is the reluctant magician's assistant.*

Jack   Here in Nowen we have a free-style alphabet, and that's the joy – you only need to know the first few sounds. After that it's entirely up to you. You see, individuality is encouraged here in Nowen. Feel free to express yourself – no matter what religion you are. Are you ready? Let's give it a go.

Jack *recites the Nowenthian Alphabet Song with the audience.*

Jack   That was fantastic. Thank you so much, or as we say in Nowen – thoo ke so moh. Do you think you could try that? You do? Brilliant!

Jack *teaches the audience to say 'thank you so much' in Nowenthian, perhaps bringing some of them up on stage to help.*

Jack   Now I need to talk to you about Daisy. We are aware that due to the recent bout of earwig flu all farm animals are being slaughtered, but Daisy's been with us for years. And without her milk to sell, we won't be able to survive. Will you help us hide her? You will? Oh, thoo ke so moh. If we ever get a visit from the not so nice Inspector Thorgulund Thrushp please don't say a word. Right, it's time, it's Tupperware time, and if it's Tupperware time, it's time to meet my mum, Tupperware Tina . . .

Dame (*entering*)   Hello, it's me – Tupperware Tina! And who loves Tupperware? (*Audience – We do!*) Who loves Tupperware? (*Audience – We do!*) Wonderful. Now let me take a good look at you. Hello, sir, I can see by the size of your membez[16] that you have travelled a great distance to be here. Lovely to see you again, madam. Best to keep your Tupperware under your jimmy bassildons[17] this time, we don't want a repeat of last year. And, who knows, if you're very good I might let you taste a cucuppski[18] of my delicious herbal bishop.[19] Welcome to Tupperware Tina's Top Tips – yes I did say tips, madam! Now, it's Tupperware evaluation time and who knows, maybe this year we'll find the missing part of my Rhombus Podge.[20] (*She shows her necklace which has a Tupperware lid dangling on it and we hear a sound effect 'Sister, sister'.*) So who's brought their Tupperware with them today/ tonight. Let's have a show of Tupperware, please? But . . . who will be first? Will it be you, sir, you, madam, or you, or you or you, you, you, you or you?! Here in Nowen, there's only one way to decide. A quick round of . . . (*Drumroll.*) Japperson Queg.[21] (*Sound effect of a crowd going wild.*) It's so simple to play: when I say Japperson, you say Queg. Oh yeah, when I say Japperson, you say Queg. Ready? Japperson.

Jack *with audience*   Queg.

Dame   Japperson.

---

[16] An inflatable shoulder.
[17] Secretive erogenous zone with frilly hems – the 'J' spot.
[18] Unit of measurement used predominantly for measuring kitchen units.
[19] An extremely potent aphrodisiac favoured and flavoured by campanologists.
[20] Allegedly one of earliest Tupperware relics dating back and forward to the reign of Gary the Rubbish Plumber.
[21] Similar to the game rock, paper, scissors but not really.

Jack *with audience*   Queg.

Dame   Japperson.

Jack *with audience*   Queg.

Dame   Japperson.

Jack *with audience*   Queg.

Etc. Getting faster and faster, ending in a crescendo of noise and silly gestures.

Dame   It's you!

The **Dame** *points and looks at the winner.* **Jack** *is also looking at the winner but is pointing at the sky – the* **Dame** *notices this and gently guides his point towards the winner.*

Dame   What's your name and where d'you come from?

Audience Member Two   I'm Jebby Dobson from Upper Smenth[22] (*Sound effect of whooping crowds.* **Jebby** *enthusiastically waves to the audience.*)

Dame   Now what have you got for us today, Jebby? (*Taking the round piece of Tupperware into her hands.*) Wow, a spectacular piece!

Audience Member Two   Thank you, my mother found it amongst my grandfather's collection of cheesey bibbles[23] while she was dusting his frobishers.[24]

Dame   I imagine she was, Jebby, and who can blame her, it's a beauty. Do you have the jebby, Jebby? Are you aware that in ancient Nowenthian your name, Jebby,[25] means 'lid'?

Audience Member Two   Yes.

Dame   Great.

---

[22] Small desert dessert village made entirely of soufflé.
[23] Less tasty than omelette groove bubbles and more flammable than a sachet of Sue Barkers' butter bits.
[24] Motionless erotic dance routine performed with extreme prejudice and optional earmuffs.
[25] A lid, see also lid. Lid enthusiasts should consult Mother Theresa's 'Religious Iconography and Lids for Dummies'.

Jebby *produces the lid from his bag. It's a much smaller square one.*

Dame   Hmm. I'm sorry to tell you this is not actually the original jebby, Jebby.

Audience Member Two   Oh!

Dame   You can see from the markings on the back it was manufactured in Sho-Felsg.[26] Possibly early Flom Flobs.[27] Of course, if you had the original jebby, Jebby, we'd be talking forty, forty-five hundred Johnsons.[28] As is, I'd still advise you to insure it for at least three hundred.

Audience Member Two   Crembez![29] That's a lot of moonsause.[30]

Dame   And let's just have a quick check? (*She tries to match the piece to her necklace; finding this match clearly means a lot to her – repeat of the 'Sister, sister' sound effect.*) No. (*Sad but the show must go on.*) Who's up next? Japperson.

Jack (*with audience*)   Queg.

Dame   Japperson.

Jack (*with audience*)   Queg.

Dame   Japperson.

Jack (*with audience*)   Queg.

Etc. Getting faster and faster. If any audience members have brought in Tupperware the **Dame** *will now give them an improvised evaluation followed by a prize for coming up on stage. Then . . .*

Dame   There's possibly time for just one more. Japperson.

Jack (*with audience*)   Queg. (*Etc.*)

---

[26] An undiscovered extinct island that is geographically and spiritually always late.
[27] An era that is and was unavailable for comment.
[28] Quenteth, johnsons – varying denominations for Nowenthian currency; a Johnson being worth about 64.35678 quenteths depending on shoe size.
[29] A flexible exclamation keen on yoga.
[30] Any type of currency. Always read the label.

Dame (*pointing at the winner*) It's you! (*Again* **Jack** *fails to point in the right direction.*) What's your name and where do you come from?

Audience Member Three Johnny Forsyth[31] from the Moonjabas.

They instantly dance and sing an excerpt of 'Bishy Boshy Fishcakes'[32] from the Moonjabas' first album 'Quench Your Cleves'[33] then immediately continue as if nothing had happened.

Dame (*taking the large piece of Tupperware into her hands*) And what do we have here?

Audience Member Three She's been in the family for years.

Dame And an absolute belter she is. Early Louis Pompøms,[34] I think. Now, if I may. (*Checking if it's the matching piece, 'Sister, sister'—no luck.*) Do you have a pair?

Audience Member Three Yes. (*Produces a pear.*)

Dame Fantastic. So do I. (*Produces another pear.*) You take this pair, well done.

Audience Member Three, *confused, is shown to their seat.*

Dame Thoo ke so moh, ladies and gentlemen. Who loves Tupperware?

Audience We do. (*Etc.*)

Scene Three

Deep in the Gazoobian Mountains

Narrator The grounds of the Workhouse, later that night. An eerie atmosphere pervades . . .

---

[31] Founders and Keepers of the Bruce Forsyth Saga Holiday Memorial Fund (FAKOTBFSHMF)

[32] The only song ever recorded to include Dimitri Johnson's diminished seventh postulated above the fifth, without rye. Must be played with quiche.

[33] The ability to outlive numerous wives of bad tempered, bad bearded English monarchs.

[34] A camp period of Gallic flourishing.

*Some of the other actors take it upon themselves to contribute with sounds effects, a makeshift bat flies across the stage. The **Narrator** will try to suppress them if they go too far.*

Narrator   Geoff, the smallest giant in the world, is sleeping. Grenthel enters carrying a box of matches, a locket and the bluepr . . .

Grenthel (*out of character*)   . . . we can't find the locket!

Narrator   Carrying a box of matches and the blueprints to the building.

Grenthel   Geoff.

She strikes a match and lights a candle. The stage lights come up simultaneously, but far too bright.

Geoff   Wow, that's a bright candle!

Grenthel   Yes it is. I'll just shield it a bit.

Gestures for the lighting operator to turn it down. The lighting then dips down to almost black.

I'll just shield it a bit less.

Finally the lights come up to the correct level.

Geoff   That's better!

Grenthel   I've got the blueprints.

She unrolls the plans.

Grenthel   The ventilation system, see it goes past here and then down . . .

Geoff   . . . the pipes are right over our heads but there's no way in.

Grenthel   There!

Geoff   What?

Grenthel   The access hatch.

Geoff Beyond the Door of Doom!

Grenthel Let's do it! Sometimes in life you have to face your fears – no matter what religion you are.

Geoff Right, let's go. Blow out the candle.

They both look slightly towards the stage manager position to ensure that they're ready. **Grenthel** *blows out the candle. Two seconds later the lights snap to black.*

Scene Four

Up in the Clouds

An ethereal 'Ah-Ah-Ah-Ah' resounds. Figures with a white beards, dressed in mariachi outfits appear through the smoke (all are dressed in the same way throughout the play).

Shepherd Ban Ki Who's there?

Shepherd Boutros Nay, answer me. Stand and unfold yourself.

Shepherd Ban Ki Long live The Shepherds Gonzalez!

Shepherd Boutros Ban Ki?

Shepherd Ban Ki He.

Shepherd Dave Hello?

Shepherd Boutros Dave?

Shepherd Dave Where's Kofi and Gary?

Shepherd Boutros On their way up.

Shepherd Ban Ki They've been down there again?

Shepherd Boutros Last week a Gazoobian got his bishops stuck in a flasb.[35] Yesterday a Nowenthian needed spiritual guidance. It's about time we oracles had a proper crisis to solve.

---

[35] A farmyard implement yet to be implemented.

Shepherd Dave   I think I hear them!

Shepherd Boutros   Stand, ho! Who's there?

Shepherd Kofi   Friends to this ground.

Shepherd Gary   And liegemen to the Shepherds.

Shepherd Boutros   Kofi! Gary!

Shepherd Kofi   Boutros!

Shepherd Ban Ki   What's happening down in the land of Waa?

Shepherd Kofi   Code Purple!

Shepherds Gary, Boutros *and* **Ban Ki**   Code Purple!

Shepherd Ban Ki   Remind me again what a Code Purple is?

Shepherd Gary   It's a mixture of a Code Red and a Code Blue.

Shepherd Ban Ki   Oh, right! (*Beat.*) So what is that?

Shepherd Boutros   It means that people are in desperate need of . . .

All Shepherds (*striking a pose*)   The Shepherds Gonzalez! (*Ah-Ah-Ah-Ah.*)

Shepherd Kofi   Let us sing the song that every Shepherd child learns . . .

Shepherd Gary   The song to summon our powers and prepare us for the journey ahead.

SONG TWO: WE ARE THE SHEPHERDS

We are the Shepherds Gonzalez
We are Shepherds Gonzalez
We are the Shepherds Gonzalez
And we're here to help you

Whether you're a Christian, Muslim or Jew
Come and pull up a pew
Rastafarian, Buddhist or Sikh
Would you kindly take your seat

We are the Shepherds Gonzalez
We are Shepherds Gonzalez
We are the Shepherds Gonzalez
And we're here to help you

Whether you're a Christian, Muslim or Jew
Come and pull up a pew
Rastafarian, Buddhist or Sikh
Would you kindly take your seat

We are the Shepherds Gonzalez
We are Shepherds Gonzalez
We are the Shepherds Gonzalez
And we're here to help you

If you're a non religious humanist, agnostic or an atheist
A Hindu or Confusionist, a Shinto or a Mormonist
Scientologist or Paganist, a Jainist or a Spiritist
Or even Unaffiliated

You could follow any folk religion, try Korean Shamanism,
Be Primal Indigenous become Jehova's Witness
Chinese Traditional, Tao or Unitarian
No matter who you are

If you're Cao Dai, Candomble, Bahai, Juche
Badimo or Tenrikyo, Zoroastrian or Egungun
Eshu or Mingi, Ogoun or Ozi
or any of the Afro-Carribean syncretic religions
originating in Cuba – such as Santeria; also known Regla
de Lucumi . . .

We're here to help you

We are the Shepherds Gonzalez
We are Shepherds Gonzalez
We are the Shepherds Gonzalez

And we're here to help you
Yes we're here
Ban Ki – Gary – Kofi – Boutros – Dave
To help you!

The Shepherds Gonzalez *exit but* **Ban Ki** *calls back* **Gary**.

Shepherd Ban Ki   Gary? I just wondered, uh . . . I haven't
been on a mission for ages.

Shepherd Gary   Yes?

Shepherd Ban Ki   Is it because I'm . . .

Shepherd Gary   Tall?

Shepherd Ban Ki   No, no . . .

Shepherd Gary   A girl?

Shepherd Ban Ki   No, (*Pointing to face.*) you know . . .

Shepherd Gary   Oh, no of course it's not that. Oracles
aren't . . . I mean's Dave's also . . . and he's had plenty of
missions.

Shepherd Ban Ki   I know and I'm much better at parallel
wishes than him. So why?

Shepherd Gary   Alright don't get your knickers in a
ronson,[36] you're coming this time.

Shepherd Ban Ki   Thanks, Gary. I promise I won't let
you down.

Shepherd Gary (*looks out in thought, perusing the future and sees
it and smiled*)   No, you won't!

Shepherd Ban Ki   Hey, where are we going?

Shepherd Gary   Let's just say a Nowenthian farm boy will
soon need our help and two Gazoobians are about to enter
great danger. (*Beat.*) And about the other thing . . .

---

[36] Not to be confused with Mark Ronson's briefs or Jim Broadbent's slightly longer.

Shepherd Ban Ki   Yes?

Shepherd Gary   Oracles have never had an issue with false teeth.

Shepherd Ban Ki *self-consciously raises a hand to her teeth.*

Scene Five

Jack's Farmhouse in Nowen

Narrator   Meanwhile back at Jack's farm, Thorgulund Thrushp, the not so nice Inspector we mentioned earlier, was on his way . . .

Dame   Quick, hide Daisy.

Jack (*to the audience*)   Remember please, not a word.

Dame   Hurry, he's coming!

Jack   Where?

Nothing happens.

Dame   Quick the Inspector is coming.

Narrator (*Whispers into the wings.*)   Gloria? (*Or real name of actor.*)

Inspector (*enters half dressed*)   Ah ha!

Dame   How can we help you, Inspector?

Inspector   We've heard of a farm in the vicinity that is harbouring a cow.

Jack/Dame (*mock shock*)   Harbouring a cow? Who would do such a thing?

Thrushp *questions the audience on whether they have seen the cow.*

Inspector   I needn't remind you that anyone harbouring a cow or any illegal animal for that matter will be dealt with severely.

Dame   If we hear anything you'll be the first to know, Inspector.

The actor playing the **Inspector** *pauses and then looks into the* **Dame***'s eyes, trying to read for any signals about what happens next. The actor playing the* **Dame** *realises that his fellow actor has forgotten the lines and whispers for them to just 'use something from Hamlet'.*

Inspector   I must be cruel only to be kind, thus bad begins and worse remains behind.

He exits.

Jack   Mum, it's too dangerous for Daisy here. But if we get rid of her we won't have two Johnsons to rub together.

Dame   We'll get by somehow, son. Because remember, we're happy and we're poor.

They all do an over-the-top jump for joy.

Dame/Jack/Daisy   Yeah!

Jack   Why don't you start charging for your Tupperware evaluations?

Dame   No! That money's for charity.

Jack   But what about Daisy?

Dame   Son, there comes a time in everyone's life when one has to consult – The Shepherds Gonzalez (*'Ah-Ah-Ah-Ah'*).

Jack   The Shepherds Gonzalez? (*'Ah-Ah-Ah-Ah'*)

Actor (*offstage*)   They were brilliant when my Albert had trouble with his hanging Jacksons.[37]

Actor Two (*offstage*)   They helped my granny get her Tibby Tibsons[38] shiny again after years of neglect.

---

[37] Gargantuan smiley faced glands, achievable with a low impact knee brace.
[38] Formica undergarments favoured by the elderly. Frequent use leads to loss of sheen, infrequent use leads to loss of Charlie Sheen.

Jack The Shepherds Gonzalez. (*'Ah-Ah-Ah-Ah'*.) Of course!
Don't worry Daisy, we'll take you across the border to the
humble Shepherds Gonzalez. You'll be safe there.

Dame But before you go, my precious bovine beauty, a few
words of advice.
  Give thy thoughts no tongue.
  Be thou familiar, but by no means vulgar.
  Beware of entrance to a quarrel, but being in,
  Bear't that the opposed may beware of thee.

Jack *hurries the* **Dame** *off stage and she rushes to the most
important lines.*

Dame Neither a borrower nor a lender be;
  This above all: to thine own self be true.

Jack Night, night Daisy. It's going to be okay.

They exit.

SONG THREE: IF I WERE

If I were tall
Like a giraffe
Then I would look upon the world
And I would laugh
I'd see for miles
Right to the sea
I'd be the one to pick the biggest, finest fruit
From off the tree
And everybody would look up to me
And say 'oh wow'
But I'm a cow
A lowly cow
I'm just a cow

Or a bear
That would be nice
I could be brown or maybe black
Or a polar bear on ice
Well then I'd roar

'Cause I'd be strong
I'd be the one you wouldn't mess with
Unless you got it all wrong
'Cause if you wanted to pick a fight with me
Then I'd show you how
But I'm a cow
A lowly cow
I'm just a cow

Grass is always greener on the other side
And there's so much of life that's left to see
I've lost all my friends and family to
Bovine spongiform encephalopathy

If I was an anaconda
I would be fonder
Of life so close up to the ground
I'd travel here I'd travel round
And I'd be sly
Deep in the grass
I'd be a creature to avoid or else I'd
Bite you on the arse
And with my venom I could take on
Anything pow-wow
But I'm a cow
A lowly cow
I'm just a cow

Grass is always greener on the other side
And there's so much of life that's left to see
I've lost all my friends and family to
Bovine spongiform encephalopathy
BSE, yes it's clear to see
It's BSE, don't blame me
Do I hear a B? Do I hear an S? Do I hear an E?
What's that spell?
BSE . . .

You remember the time when Tesco and Waitrose were
removing all their products from the shelves and poor

farmers were having to cull their animals, oh yeah. That's right. Hard times. Hard times. Bi bap bi di di bap bo de do di da . . .

Exits scatting.

Scene Six

Deep in the Gazoobian Mountains

Jack *as* **Narrator**   Meanwhile back at the workhouse, night has fallen and brave Geoff and Grenthel make their escape.

Silence. The following is presented as if the actors playing **Grimm** *and* **Grenthel** *have left their radio microphones backstage. At one point* **Jack** *rushes off to get them.*

The sound of a door opening . . .

Grimm *(offstage, out of character)*   Paige. *(Or real name of actor.)* is that you in there?

A wee.

Grenthel *(offstage, out of character)*   Yeah.

The sound of a cubicle door opening, closing and locking.

Grimm *(offstage, out of character)*   Good audience, eh!

A fart.

Grenthel *(offstage, out of character)*   I'm not looking forward to Act Two! You know, the kiss. I think Killian *(Or real name of actor.)* ate garlic last night.

A fart.

Grimm *(offstage, out of character)*   I thought I could smell something.

Grenthel *(offstage, out of character)*   Do you think we're doing okay?

Grimm (*offstage, out of character*)   It's a bit tricky when we haven't rehearsed!

A plop.

Grenthel (*offstage, out of character*)   Any tips?

Grimm (*offstage, out of character*)   If I get stuck I find something appropriate from Hamlet. They don't even notice!

Grenthel (*offstage, out of character*)   Hm. When are we next on?

A toilet flush.

Grimm (*offstage, out of character*)   Hold on, haven't we just had the cow song?

Grenthel (*offstage, out of character*)   Oh no! It's us!

An unsuccessful toilet flush.

Grenthel (*offstage, out of character*)   It won't flush!

More attempts at flushing, doors opening and closing.

Grimm (*offstage, out of character*)   Just leave it . . .

We hear them rush out of the bathroom and down the corridor, bumping into the actor playing **Jack** *whom we hear calling out for them in the corridor. Then . . .*

Grimm *enters, a little out of breath, with a piece of toilet paper hanging out of her costume.*

Grimm (*she freezes, finally*)   Now is the very witching time of night when churchyard yawn and hell itself breaths out contagion to this world, now could I drink hot blood. But soft . . .

A door squeaks open and **Grenthel** *and* **Geoff** *enter.*

Geoff (*whispering*)   All is not well, I doubt some foul play.

The door closes behind them with a thud.

Grenthel   Look, it's over there, the access hatch.

Suddenly **Geoff** *is caught in a beam, he can't move.*

Grimm   The lovebirds. I knew it!

Grenthel   Mother!

Grimm   Stay out of this!

Geoff   Let go of me. What is this?

Grimm   I've just finished creating my latest invention. My Hemi-spherical Tupperware Force Field.[39] With this little beauty I can miniaturise anything or anyone I like into . . . a bean!

Grenthel   A bean?

Geoff   A bean?

Grimm   You didn't think this workhouse was for doing *good* did you? Oh, you silly thing. I've been grooming them all, ready to take over. Total globsk[40] domination!

Geoff   You're mad!

Grimm   I am but mad north north-west. When the wind is southerly I know a hawk from a handsaw. (*Voices changes to more colloquial.*) It's actually all very logical. You see (*Pulling down a chart/map.*) beans are our major export.

Two placards appear to each side of the stage with the word 'PLOT' hastily written on them. They move up and down a few times then disappear.

We sell them all over the globsk. By miniaturising giants into beans, wherever they go, we go too. The beans will get planted, huge beanstalks will grow and my lovely little giants will awaken at the top to wreak havoc. With all the money from your marriage I'll be able to power even more Force

---

[39] See Rudolph Stobart's impressive tome 'Adventures around my Thighs – the real story', Methuen, 74th edition.
[40] Our planet.

Field machines, miniaturising more and more giants
and sending them all over the land.

Geoff   I'll never harm anyone.

Grimm   Ah, but that's the genius of my invention. The
process has a delightful side effect; you'll become truly evil.

Grenthel   Speak no more, thou turn'st mine eyes into my
very soul.

Grimm   Oh, I'm done talking. It's time!

*The lights shake and the room rumbles. Then with a bang, the stage
plunges into darkness. Lights up and there's a bean at the centre of
the stage, where* **Geoff** *was.* **Grimm** *picks up the bean and throws it
into a huge crate of beans.* **Grenthel** *runs over to it. Picking up
different beans in her hand and looking at them . . .*

Grenthel   Geoff? (*Picking up another.*) Geoff?

Grimm   You'll never find him, Grenthel and even if you
did, he won't remember his own name let alone remember
you! Hahahahaha. (*Waving.*) Ban Ki-moon![41]

Grenthel *alone on stage.*

Grenthel (*crying*) Geoff? Geoff?

SONG FOUR: I'LL ALWAYS FIND YOU

I'll always find you, wherever you go
Even if you change your name to Hugo
Yes I will find you no matter where you are
'Cause you and I are made to be as one

I'll always find you, we'll be together
Even if you change your name to Trevor
Yes I will find you and I will hold you close
A life without my Geoff I won't abide

---

[41] Not to be confused with Ban Ki-moon the eighth and current Secretary-General of
the United Nations.

My mother, her intentions they are evil
She's treating all the giants here with hate
It's time to undertake a big upheaval
The time to act is now I cannot wait

Change your religion, learn long division
If other people look at you with mild derision
I'll still be there, Geoff, without condition
Beauty's not skin deep that much I know

I'll cross the valleys, of wheat and barley
Even if you change your name to Boutros Boutros-Ghali[42]
Yes I will find you and I will free your heart
'Cause love will always triumph in the end

I'll cross the valleys, of wheat and barley
Even if you change your name to Boutros Boutros-Ghali
Yes I will find you and I will free your heart
A life without my Geoff
Be he dumb, or blind or deaf
But life without my Geoff I can't abide

Scene Seven

The Woods near the Border

Geoff (*offstage, out of character*)   I tell you, I am *doing* the gravedigger scene!

Geoff *as* **Narrator** (*enters*)   Jack and Daisy had travelled for days. It was a treacherous journey to . . . actually I've got a costume change, I really gotta go.

To the audience.

Can someone else read this?

---

[42] Not to be confused with Boutros Boutros-Ghali the Egyptian politician and diplomat, the sixth Secretary-General of the United Nations from January 1992 to December 1996.

He pulls up a member of the audience and gets them to read the next bit into the microphone then exits.

Audience Member Four (*reading from script*)   Jack and Daisy had travelled for days. It was a treacherous journey to seek the Shepherds Gonzalez. If they were caught, Daisy would surely be for the slaughter!

Silence. Nothing happens.

Jack (*offstage, to the audience member in a stage whisper*)   Keep going. (*Pause.*) We're not ready yet. (*Pause.*) Just make something up.

Etc. to be improvised depending on the reaction of the audience member who is most likely feeling rather awkward alone on stage, finally . . .

Jack and **Daisy** *enter. They are in rubbish disguises: sunglasses, hat and trench coat.*

Jack (*out of character, to audience member*)   Thanks!

The audience member may need to return to their seat at this point or they can remain there for longer, in which case a moment will need to be found later and the comedy awkwardness of them remaining on stage can be played with.

Jack (*stops and admires the view*)   Nearly there Daisy, my leather-coated friend. Look yonder, see the sinister silhouette of the Gazoobian mountains.

Jack *points in the opposite direction to where he is clearly looking.* **Daisy** *gently guides his arm so he is eventually pointing the right way.*

Jack   Hey, I'm starving.

He takes out a piece of Tupperware. It has sandwiches in it. He pops it open. He closes it and opens it again to hear the beauteous sound once more.

Listen to that. The simple sound of Tupperware popping. Pop popperty pop pop pop pop pop.

Jack *feeds* **Daisy** *and chews on a sandwich.*

Jack Tupperware, humble Tupperware. Who loves Tupperware?

Audience We do . . . (*Etc.*)

Jack I'm really gonna miss you, Daisy but we have to do this. I'm so sorry. (*He gives* **Daisy** *a huge hug.*) We'll see each other soon, I promise. It's time. Time to cross the border.

They make to go . . .

Inspector A moment please! Do I know you?

Jack (*to* **Daisy**) The Inspector!

Inspector Hmm. I know you, yes?

Jack (*assuming an accent of one foreign to these parts*) Know? No!

Inspector No?

Jack No.

Inspector You look familiar.

Jack No.

Inspector No?

Jack No.

Inspector Stop that!

Jack No.

Inspector No?

Jack What?

Inspector May I ask what you're doing in these parts?

Jack Alright!

Inspector So . . .

Jack So?

Inspector   What?

Jack   What are you doing in these parts?

Inspector   I'm here to ask people what they are doing in these parts.

Jack   We know that. You've already asked us. Anything else?

Inspector   Er . . . Yes . . . I'm checking for dairy animals.

Jack   And have you got any?

Inspector   No, I haven't!

Jack   Awfully large penalty to pay if you had.

Inspector   That's right.

Jack   How much were you thinking?

Inspector   Twenty-five Johnsons.

Jack   Could be a problem this time of night. Let's call it thirty.

Inspector   But I've only got a fifty.

Jack   Give us that and I'll let you off the rest.

Inspector   Really? Thank you.

Jack   We're not all bad you know. Now run along.

He starts to leave and gets halfway across the stage when suddenly he stops in his tracks.

Inspector   Whoaa! Hold on a minute.

Jack   Absolutely.

Inspector   We're not done yet.

Jack   We are not!

Inspector   Who's interviewing who here?

Jack   I was just about to ask you the same thing.

Inspector Well, make it snappy.

Jack Who's interviewing who here?

Inspector I'm not sure. But there's only one way to settle it.

Jack A quick round of Japperson Queg?

Inspector Japperson?

Jack Queg!

Inspector Japperson.

Jack Queg.

Inspector Japperson.

Jack Queg! (*Etc.*) We'll be on our way then.

Inspector Hang on, who's she?

Jack This is my girlfriend.

Inspector Looks like a cow.

Jack How dare you. (*Slap.*)

Inspector It's her udder.

Jack Her udder what?

Inspector Her udder.

Jack You've said that twice.

Inspector She looks like a cow.

Jack Right charmer you are. (*Slap.*)

Inspector Didn't mean to offend.

Jack Honestly. Insulting my lady like this!

Inspector Like what?

Jack Like this. (*Slap.*)

Inspector Ouch!

Jack Let's not argue. Shall we dance?

Inspector I'd love to. Haven't danced in ages.

They dance.

Inspector Why are we dancing?

They stop.

Jack Are you asking?

Inspector Yes, I am.

Jack Then I'm dancing.

They start dancing again.

Daisy What a piece of work is man, how noble in reason, how infinite in faculty.

Jack *and the* **Inspector** *suddenly stop and look at* **Daisy** *in disbelief.* **Daisy** *moos.*

Inspector Was that a cow?

Jack I've already warned you once!

Inspector Right, well you be on your way then.

Jack I will.

Inspector And where's that?

Jack (*pointing one way but looking the other*)   First right. Straight ahead and left at the tree.

Inspector Thank you very much. (*Exits.*)

Jack That was close!

A figure appears from a puff of smoke.

Shepherd Gary I am a Shepherd Gonzalez (*'Ah-Ah-Ah-Ah'.*)

Jack So it's true. You do come with your own theme tune.

Shepherd Gary (*Singing to the tune 'Ah-Ah-Ah-Ah'.*)   Ye-e-e-es. Now what can I do for you, Jack?

Jack How do you know my name?

Shepherd Gary I know everything.

Jack Really. Okay how many fingers am I holding up behind my back?

Jack *holds up three fingers.*

Shepherd Gary Three.

Jack What, how did you . . . ? (*Breaking character.*) That's actually really good, Paige. (*Or real name of actor.*)

Shepherd Gary (*out of character*) I know. Thanks.

Jack (*out of character*) No, how did you do that?

Shepherd Gary (*out of character*) Method acting. Three weeks with Derren Brown.

Jack (*out of character*) You reckon you could do it to anyone?

Shepherd Gary (*out of character*) Yep.

Jack (*out of character, to the audience*) Who would like a go? Anyone want to test the skills of a true Shepherd Gonzalez? (*'Ah-Ah-Ah-Ah'.*)

Jack *gets a few volunteers from the audience and each time* **Shepherd Gary** *gets the number of fingers right; this is achieved by the actors learning twelve lines corresponding to numbers which the actor playing* **Jack** *will use to feed the answer.*

0] I like it, I like it.
1]You'll never get this one.
2] Okay I'm saying nothing.
3] Nothing, actor stands with lips sealed gesture.
4] Come on, this is supposed to be easy.
5] Can the Shepherd get it right?
6] The suspense is killing me.
7] Time to guess.
8] That's a good 'un.

9] Tricky one for you.

10] Ah hah!

Same as the previous one] Nice!

At the end of this sequence, the final participant returns to their seat.

Jack Wow, you really are a Shepherd Gonzalez. (*'Ah-Ah-Ah-Ah'.*)

Shepherd Gary How can I help?

Jack It's Daisy, our cow. The recent bout of earwig flu has meant the . . .

Shepherd Gary . . . slaughter of farmyard animals, yes, I know.

Jack But Daisy, she's like family. She's my best friend. Would you be prepared to harbour her until this senseless slaughter ceases?

Shepherd Gary No problem.

Jack Easy as that?

Shepherd Gary Dispensation of knowledge, random acts of kindness . . .

Jack Random acts of kindness, wow!

Shepherd Gary Yep, that's us!

Jack Us?

Shepherd Gary It's not just me. No, no, no, there's five of us.

Jack Five?

Shepherd Gary We're on a rota. I do Thursdays, Saturdays and every other 47th Tuesday unless we've got band practice.

Jack You're in a band?

Shepherd Gary All part of being an oracle these days. Oracle Directive 32b 'Oracles must communicate across all media'. Quite fun actually, we've done a few gigs. Birthdays, bat mitzvahs, Hindu weddings, that sort of thing. Got to cater for all the religions nowadays. An oracle can't be secular anymore.

Jack Really? Hmm . . .

Shepherd Gary *and* **Daisy** *start to exit, their 'exit' being live on stage with* **Shepherd Gary** *covering his mouth to make an off-in-the-distance sound effect as he gets further away.*

Shepherd Gary (*in the distance*) There are more things in heaven and earth, Jack, than are dreamed of in your philosophy.

Jack Pardon?

Shepherd Gary (*further in the distance*) You will find the answer in the sky.

Jack What do you mean?

Shepherd Gary (*further still*) Remember me . . .

Jack What?

Shepherd Gary (*out of character*) Yeah, I've really got to go now.

Scene Eight

Deep in the Gazoobian Mountains

Grimm *holds a large telephone that is connected with all sorts of wires through a big transformer onto a bicycle, which one of the giants is peddling. Odd noises and beeps, possibly a light on the phone. Her hair is puffed out like it's been electrocuted.*

Jack (**Hamlet**) To be . . .

Dame (*out of character*) Don't even think about it!

Jack (*out of character*) But Michael . . . (*Or real name of actor.*)

Dame (*out of character*)   Just set the scene!

Jack *as* **Narrator**   The workhouse!

Exits.

Grimm   The wedding cake? Yes, first thing Monday. The pastel pansies? Absolutely!

Does a round and round she's-going-on-and-on gesture, which the giant interprets as an instruction to pedal harder.

That's right, Queen Melody. Soon our two families will be united (*Aside.*) and I'll get my hands on *all* your money! (*Sweet.*) Grenthel? She's delighted. Ban Ki-moon.

She hangs up.

Grimm   Imbecile! Ah this is so easy. I'll finally get my revenge on those wicked giants. I'll teach them not to steal little girls.

SONG FIVE: MY PLAN

I made a plan
I would have riches through the world
And all the boys and girls
and everyone would bow to me

I made a plan
I would send giants out to work
They'd go berserk
And they'd wreak havoc just for me

I made a plan
That we would marry into money
Think it's funny
Then you'll have to step aside and weep

I made a plan
In three days I'll have more power
Men will cower
And they'll bow down just to me

It's easy to achieve world domination
It's fun to watch worlds crumble at your feet
Without a single scrap of trepidation
'Cause when the music stops it won't be me without a seat

I made a plan
I don't care you don't approve
You think I'm rude?
You think I'll come good in the end? [No!]

Oh not not I
I've waited years enough for this
I will not kiss
I will not beg you have to fight to win

It's easy to achieve world domination
It's fun to watch worlds crumble at your feet
Without a single scrap of trepidation
'Cause when the music stops it won't be me without a seat

How could it be?
That my daughter she is so good
She should be rude
She should be evil just like me

Well nevermind
For come next week she'll be of use
She's so obtuse
I guess then all the money will be mine
[Oh yes I like that] All the money will be mine
[Ooh yes that's good] All the money will be mine!

A **Giant** *runs on and cowers before her.*

Giant Messenger   I'm sorry, Ms Grimm.

Grimm   What is it?

Giant Messenger   It's your daughter.

Grimm   Does the dress not fit?

Giant Messenger   It's not that. She's . . . gone.

Grimm   What?

Giant Messenger   She was just spotted leaving on Juju bird flight.

Grimm   Domestic or international?

Giant Messenger   International.

Grimm (*cursing*)   Eddie Stobart! Without her, I get nothing. I'll fetch her back – where did she go?

Giant Messenger   To Nowen.

Grimm   Nowen, heh? The spiritual home of Tupperware! Every cloud has a silver Johnson!

Scene Nine

The Market Place in Nowen

Geoff (*breaking character, at the narrator position*)   The market, where I finally get to do the gravedigger scene! Yes!

Jack and **Dame** *are at the market, the scene is set by the other actors.*

Actor A   Beans, beans for sale! Green beans, black beans, runner beans, kidney beans, has beans, wanna beans. (*Etc.*)

Actor B   Fresh Gwenth.[43] None finer in the whole of Waa. Get your Gwenth. (*Etc.*)

Actor C   Tug of Jepson,[44] Sir? Try your hand at 'The Throwing of the Gottang'.[45] (*Etc.*)

Dame   Jack. Is Daisy okay?

Jack   She's safe. Safe with the Shepherds Gonzalez (*Audience respond*). What's wrong?

Dame   It's nothing.

---

[43] Stale plonth (a delicacy).
[44] Your choice but please use your imagination responsibly.
[45] The Gottang – an invisible egg whisk shaped egg whisk rarely used in the whisking of eggs.

Jack Mother, please.

Dame We can't pay the rent. One week, then we're being evicted.

Jack One week? What are we going to do?

Suddenly epic theme music blares out . . .

Announcer (*V/O*) Welcome to the 64th Annual Bunger Games. Do we have a contender from District Pillipots?

Bishy McGwendez *steps up.*

Announcer (*V/O*) Bishy McGwendez, last year's winner, has volunteered! Do we have a contender from District Nowen?

Jack *raises his hand.*

Dame No, Jack!

Jack Mum, we have to win the moonsause.

Dame No, Jack, you can't.

Jack It's the only way, Mum.

Dame But if you lose . . .!

Announcer (*V/O*) It's time for the Tug of Jepson. Players, select your team.

Jack *and* **Bishy** *select their half of the audience.*

Dame Those of you new to this, here's how it works. Each player will tug on the Jepson. When the team gets closer to *you,* (*One side of theatre.*) you all shout 'Jeppy peppy jeppy peppy' and when closer to *you,* (*Other side of theatre.*) you all shout 'Soh-nny – soh-nny'.

Commentator One (*V/O*) Well, the Tug of Joh-hepson, one of the earliest non-contact sports from Nowen. The Tug of the Jepson, of course, derived from that very sport.

Commentator Two (*V/O*) And the players are ready.

The game is performed and the audience react appropriately. As
Jack *is losing . . . a figure appears from a puff of smoke. Freeze.*

Shepherd Ban Ki   Back in the game. A random act of
kindness!

Unfreeze. Unseen by anyone else, **Shepherd Ban Ki** *uses magic
powers to help* **Jack** *win.*

Announcer *(V/O)*   Congratulations. Now it's time for the
Throwing of the Gottang.

Bishy McGwendez *takes his position and starts to warm up,
stretching etc.* **Jack** *does likewise. Both await their throw . . .*

Commentator One *(V/O)*   Bishy McGwendez, of course, no
stranger to the throwing of the Gottang. And what a great
start he's had to the season.

Commentator Two *(V/O)*   Well, Jack Spriggins, the
newcomer. One would imagine the odds stacked firmly
against him on this one, John?

Commentator One *(V/O)*   Well, so much of the game now
psychological and McGwendez will surely have the
advantage there.

Bishy McGwendez *places his hands in chalk for extra grip.*

Commentator One *(V/O)*   Well, there's the rub!

Commentator Two *(V/O)*   The rub, of course, only recently
introduced into the game!

Commentator One *(V/O)*   Rub a dub dub. A rubby dubby
dibber. Three men in a tubby tibby tub tub.

Bishy *prepares. The crowd hush. He throws the (imaginary)
Gottang then, a few seconds later, catches it behind his back. The
crowd applauds, then hush. The* **Umpire** *holds up the score.*

Commentator One *(V/O)*   Seven point two, not a great
score. But certainly not the worst.

Commentator Two (*V/O*)   He'll be disappointed with that in the locker room.

Commentator One (*V/O*)   Jack Spriggins now, with perhaps the slightest of chances.

Jack *prepares. The crowd hush.*

Dame   I love you, Jack!

Umpire   Quiet please.

Jack *goes to throw the Gottang. Freeze. Spotlight on* **Shepherd Ban Ki**.

Shepherd Ban Ki   A further act of kindness.

Unfreeze. **Jack** *throws the Gottang. As it leaves his hand,* **Shepherd Ban Ki** *can be seen controlling the moves. Finally* **Jack** *catches it perfectly. The crowd applauds. The* **Umpire** *holds up the score.*

Commentator One (*V/O*)   Eight point three.

Commentator Two (*V/O*)   And he's done it. Jack Spriggins, the unseeded, the unknown, the unthinkable has happened! What a remarkable achievement, just twenty-one years of age and surely now there's great things ahead for this young man.

Dame   Jack, we've won!

Umpire (*handing* **Jack** *a coin*)   Congratulations, young sir.

Jack   Three Johnsons! That's not a lot of moonsause. We need to invest!

Dame   Invest in what?

Jack   In beans!

Dame   You mean cast off the shackles of our dairy-centric existence and move into a predominantly bean based modus operandi?

Jack   Exactly! And that investment starts right now!

Geoff (*out of character, entering*)   I'm really excited about this bit.

To the audience member who is holding the skull.

Could I have the skull please?

Dame (*out of character*)   I can't believe I'm allowing you doing this!

Shepherd Ban Ki (*out of character*)   Now Killian, (*Or real name of actor.*) as the gravedigger, will perform the bean seller scene.

Jack *looks at* **Shepherd Ban Ki** *and points at himself.* **Shepherd Ban Ki** *is confused so* **Jack** *rushes over and whispers something . . .*

Shepherd Ban Ki (*out of character*)   Oh right, and then Omar (*Or real name of actor.*) will do 'that speech' from *Hamlet*.

Jack *smiles and continues with the scene.*

Jack   I will speak to this fellow.

Jack *approaches* **Geoff,** *now the* **Beanseller,** *who caresses the skull in his hand.*

Beanseller   Do you know me, my lord?

Jack   Excellent well. You are a bean seller.

Beanseller   Not I, my lord. I am a gravedigger.

Jack   Bean seller!

Beanseller   Gravedigging bean seller.

Jack   Whose beans are these sirrah?

Beanseller   Mine, sir. (*Sings and does a silly dance.*) With a hey nonny nonny and a hey nonny nonny. You singest not Sir and therefore they are not *yours.*

Jack   What man dost own the beans?

Beanseller   No man, Sir.

Jack   What woman, then?

Beanseller   None neither.

Jack   How absolute the knave is. We must speak by the book. Where be they from these beans?

Beanseller   Imported, from the giant mountains of Gazoob.

Jack   How many seasons will they last?

Beanseller   They will last ye some eight year or nine year: a lentil or a chickpea will last ye more.

Jack   How many can I get for three Johnsons?

Beanseller   For three Johnsons – only one! And that's me being generous. Go one then, pick.

Jack *chooses a bean, changes his mind, returns it, picks another, returns it then finally settles on the one he wants. It's a little larger than the others. As he lifts it up it we hear a rumbled echo of the Fee Fi Fo Fum workhouse song –* **Jack***, however, hears it not.*

Jack (*happy with his choice*)   Thanks!

The **Beanseller** *exits, taking a bow to the audience.* **Jack** *is now alone, the lights change, a spotlight on him. His moment has arrived. He is now the classically-trained Shakespearean 'actor'. He begins to plant his bean centre stage.*

Jack   To bean or not to bean, that is the question.

Whether 'tis nobler in the mind to suffer the slings and arrows of outrageous beanstalks . . .

Suddenly he's interrupted as the lights go out and he's left in the dark.

Jack   Oh not fair! Really, really not fair!

We hear him walk off very upset.

A rumbling of the earth and the sound of a massive bean stalk growing.

Act Two

The actors walk out to chat with the audience, out of character, before the house lights go down. A couple of the actors return all of the props/costumes they had borrowed from audience members at the start (note: there won't be an opportunity for this later), others chat generally about how it's all been going, perhaps one of the actors needs help reapplying makeup. Dialogue should be improvised along the lines of:

Grenthel (*out of character*)   You were all absolutely amazing in Act One.

Jack (*out of character*)   You guys were fantastic.

Geoff (*out of character*)   Did we do okay?

Dame (*out of character*)   We couldn't have done it without you.

Grimm (*out of character*)   I'm not too scary as Ms Grimm, am I?

Dame (*out of character*)   The thing is there's only five of us, so we *are* going to need some more help in Act Two.

Stage Manager   Okay thank you, that's clearance.

Dame (*out of character*)   Standby for Act Two!

Jack (*out of character*)   Could someone please hold this again? (*Passing the skull of Yorrick.*) We might need it later. Our little secret, eh? You look like you've got a secret or two. Right, let's do this. The readiness is all.

He exits.

Grenthel (*out of character, left alone on stage*)   There's just one thing. (*Checking the coast is clear.*) I really, really love that 'Who loves Tupperware? We do' bit, but I never get to say it! Would it be okay if I had a go? (*Audience react.*) It would? That's amazing. Thank you. (*Runs off stage excitedly, then runs back on.*) Who loves Tupperware?

Audience   We do.

Grenthel (*out of character*)   Who loves Tupperware?

Audience   We do.

Stage Manager (*calling out*)   Can you clear the stage please, Paige. (*Or real name of actor.*)

Grenthel (*out of character*)   Just one more! Who loves Tupperware?

Audience   We do.

Grenthel (*out of character*)   Thanks, that was awesome!
She rushes off.

Scene One

The Woods near the Border

Narrator   The woods near the border Nowen.

REPRISE: WHEREVER YOU GO

[Grenthel]   I'll always find you, wherever you go
  Even if you change your name to Hugo
  Yes I will find you no matter where you are
  'Cause you and I are made to be as one

  Searching the whole land, I'm trying so hard
  I'll still find you if your name is Eddie Stobart
  Yes I will find you and I will hold you close
  A life without my Geoff I won't abide . . .

A figure appears from a puff of smoke.

Shepherd Dave   I am a Shepherd Gonzalez (*'Ah-Ah-Ah-Ah'.*)
I see your future: love, children, Tupperware.

Grenthel   Pardon?

Shepherd Dave   That's what most people want from an oracle nowadays, quick glimpse at the future, few hints at their destiny, that sort of thing.

Grenthel   Great, can you help me with something?

Shepherd Dave   Ask away. There's nothing I haven't heard before!

Grenthel   I'm trying to track down the destination of a crate of beans.

Shepherd Dave   No, that's a first!

Grenthel   I've got the dispatch note here.

Shepherd Dave (*taking the dispatch note*)   Hold on a minute, I'll get you the address.

He exits.

Grenthel *waits* . . . **Shepherd Kofi** *enters.*

Grenthel   Have you got it?

Shepherd Kofi   Got what?

Grenthel   The address?

Shepherd Kofi   What address?

Grenthel   The address of the crate.

Shepherd Kofi   What crate?

Grenthel   I just gave it to you.

Shepherd Kofi   Oh. That must have been Dave.

Grenthel   Dave?

Shepherd Kofi   I'll go get him.

Exits. **Grenthel** *waits* . . . **Shepherds Ban Ki** *and* **Boutros** *enter.*

Grenthel   So?

Shepherd Ban Ki   So what?

Grenthel   Where is it?

Shepherd Boutros   Where's what?

Grenthel You're kidding?

Shepherd Ban Ki Kidding about what?

Grenthel You just left.

Shepherd Boutros Left where?

Grenthel Left here.

Shepherd Boutros When?

Grenthel A minute ago.

Shepherd Boutros Oh, that must have been Kofi and Dave.

Shepherds Kofi *and* **Dave** *enter.*

Grenthel What is this?

Shepherd Boutros A rehearsal hopefully.

Grenthel A rehearsal, for what?

Shepherd Ban Ki Our band!

Shepherd Boutros Because we are The Shepherds Gonzalez.

All Shepherds (*with audience*) Ah-Ah-Ah-Ah.

Grenthel There's four of you?

Shepherd Dave Five actually.

Grenthel Where's the other one?

An awkward pause. **Grenthel** *realises that, with only a cast of four and five* **Shepherds Gonzalez,** *it must be her. She rushes off stage for a quick change.*

Grenthel Oh, look, I think she's over there . . .

The **Shepherds** *walk out to the audience and start chatting, improvising, as they wait. Then* **Shepherd Gary** *enters, a little too quickly dressed and half hanging out.*

Shepherd Gary   Here I am!

Another awkward moment as they realise that now there's no one to play **Grenthel**.

Shepherd Dave (*out of character, to the audience*)   Can someone play Grenthel for this scene, please?

The **Stage Manager** *hands an audience member a script, puts a wig on them and helps them with their lines if necessary.*

Shepherd Dave   Here you go, Grenthel. I looked up the destination of your package and have narrowed it down to the southern fields of Nowen.

Audience Member Five   Why thank you kind, fair, intelligent and incredibly handsome Shepherd Gonzalez.

All   Ah-Ah-Ah-Ah.

Audience Member Five (*reading lines*)   Before I go, I'd really like to hear the new song by the Shepherds Gonzalez. It's from their first album entitled: The Greatest Hits of the Shepherds Gonzalez.

The **Shepherds** *all act coy and surprised.*

Shepherd Boutros   No, no, please we couldn't. I'm sure you're only just saying that.

Audience Member Five (*reading lines*)   Yes, I am only just saying that because it's written here. If you want my real opinion . . .

Shepherd Boutros (*interrupting*)   . . . Okay, okay if you insist.

Audience Member Five (*reading lines*)   I'm not really insisting, I'm just . . .

Shepherd Boutros (*interrupting again and grabbing script off the audience member and quickly ushering them back to their seat*)   Alright, alright point taken. Give someone a moment in the limelight and they just can't help themselves!

SONG SIX: JUST CALL OUT OUR NAME

Doesn't matter what's buggin'
If you need a little lovin'
When you want a little huggin'
Just call out our name

Doesn't matter if you're teary
If you're feeling rather weary
When life is cold and dreary
Just call out our name

We are the Shepherds Gonzalez
The Shepherd Gonza-le-e-e-e-ez
We are the Shepherds Gonzalez
The Shepherd Gonza-le-ez

We are the Shepherd Gonza-a-a-a-a-a-a-a
le-e-e-e-e-e-e-ez
We're your Oracles
Just call out our name

Doesn't matter what's buggin'
If you need a little lovin'
When you want a little huggin'
Just call out our name

Doesn't matter if you're teary
If you're feeling rather weary
When life is cold and dreary
Just call out our name

We are the Shepherds Gonzalez
The Shepherd Gonza-le-e-e-e-ez
We are the Shepherds Gonzalez
The Shepherd Gonza-le-ez
We are the Shepherd Gonza-a-a-a-a-a-a-a
le-e-e-e-e-e-e-ez
We're your Oracles
Just call out our name

Shepherd Dave   It's so great to see all you lovely people with us this morning/afternoon/evening. Let me take a moment to introduce the band. On Snare Pods,[46] give it up for – Ban Ki-moonlight (**Ban Ki** *does a little solo*.) On Double Dobson[47] it's Kofi[48] 'our nan' Renoir (**Kofi** *does a little solo*.). On Acoustic Pops[49] – big up for Boutrous 'the nose' Ghali (**Boutros** *does a little solo*.). On Strum-Digglers[50] – Gary 'good goose' Gossling (**Gary** *does a little solo*.).

Shepherd Boutros   And of course on lead vocals – Dave Patel! (**Dave** *does a little solo*.)

Shepherd Kofi   And together we are The Shepherds Gonzalez!
 We are the Shepherds Gonzalez
 The Shepherd Gonza-le-e-e-e-ez
 We are the Shepherds Gonzalez
 The Shepherd Gonza-le-ez
 We are the Shepherd Gonza-a-a-a-a-a-a-a
 le-e-e-e-e-e-e-ez
 We're your Oracles
 Just call out our name
 We're your Oracles
 Just call out our name

Shepherd Ban Ki   Gosh, after all that singing I could really do with a sweet to soothe my throat and provide me with a short lived complex cardohydrate sugar buzz. A sweet like Sammy's Sensational Super Suckers. But alas I don't have any.

Shepherd Kofi   Then what an incredible stroke of luck it is that I happen to have a tub of Sammy's Sensational Super Suckers right here.

---

[46] Musical earmuffs.

[47] Not as aggressive as a single Dobson but certainly worth a go.

[48] Not to be confused with Kofi Atta Annan the Ghanaian diplomat who served as the seventh Secretary-General of the United Nations from January 1997 to December 2006.

[49] High socks worn between the thigh and the knee.

[50] Silent harmonious crisps that only produce quavers.

Shepherd Boutros   Sammy's Sensational Super Suckers! Then let us all enjoy this confectionery classic.

Kofi *hands them out to the* **Shepherds** *who really enjoy eating them.*

Shepherd Kofi   Oh look, it seems we have a few spare. Now what should I do with these?

All Shepherds   Oracle Directive 37b in triplicate – an Oracle always shares. Because . . . sharing is good!

They all do a double thumbs up to the audience.

Sweetie throw.

Narrator   Having met the incredibly handsome Shepherds, Grenthel continues in her quest and proceeds to the southern fields of Nowen to find her true love Geoff. Meanwhile . . .

Scene Two

Jack's Farmhouse in Nowen

Narrator   In Nowen, with the crops failing, Jack, his mum and the villagers grow hungry. But they're still happy.

All (*half hearted*)   Yeah!

Narrator   Really happy!

All (*a little less half hearted*)   Yeah!

Narrator   Really, really ha . . .

All   Easy/Don't push it.

Dame   This investment of yours isn't working. That bean has produced nothing but a giant rotten beanstalk.

The **Dame** *gestures a tiny pot plant on the stage.*

Jack (*out of character*)   It's supposed to be massive. I mean come on!

Grimm (*offstage, out of character*)   I told you we shouldn't be doing this without the props, Michael! (*Or real name of actor.*)

Stage Manager (*offstage*)   If you give me a minute we can probably . . . just need to . . . hold on . . . programme the lights and . . .

The **Assistant Stage Manager** *enters. He places a small stick in the pot and ties the plant to it, to help it stand upright. It's immediately taller, though of course still tiny!*

Stage Manager (*offstage*)   Lisa (*Or real name of Assistant Stage Manager.*) is that one in channel seventeen?

Assistant Stage Manager (*looking up to the grid*) Yeah, I think so.

Stage Manager (*offstage*)   Great . . . and sound . . . right . . . okay, we're good. Let's try that again, please. Michael (*Or real name of actor.*) can we pick it up from 'This investment of yours isn't working'. Thank you.

Dame   This investment of yours isn't working. That bean has produced nothing but a giant rotten beanstalk.

Lights dim apart from a piercing spotlight on the tiny beanstalk, powerful and spooky chords strike.

Jack (*the actor himself not being convinced*)   Wow, you're right, it's huge!

Dame   It's massive, it's rotten, it's sucking all the good out of the land. Oh, this time tomorrow we'll be out on the streets.

Jack   That's going to make it even worse at school!

Dame   Worse? Why, what's wrong?

Jack   Nobody's talking to me.

Dame   Nobody?

Jack Not even Sebusian 'baby tips' Nobson.[51]

Dame Not even Sebusian 'baby tips' Nobson?!

An actor runs onstage.

Actor Rosencrantz and Guildenstern are dead.

He runs off.

Jack Oh Mum, something's going on. All the crops in the neighbouring fields have died and people are getting ill. Sebusian's gran's got a dimmock[52] the size of a lollyped[53] right under her floombass[54] and Old Barry Bishop the carpet juggler has developed an awful rash on his jimmy dodgums.[55]

Dame Poor Barry. Now that you mention it, my gollybobbles[56] are playing up are the moment and I can't even describe what came out of my Hack-knee nibble[57] last night.

Jack Something is rotten in the state of Nowen.

Dame When sorrows come they come not single spies but in battalions.

Jack I've failed you, Mother.

Dame Nonsense, Jack. You're the brightest star in my sky.

An ethereal 'Ah–Ah-Ah-Ah'.

Jack What did you say?

Dame You're the brightest star in my sky.

An ethereal 'Ah-Ah-Ah-Ah'.

---

[51] Eventually married Maureen Hobs and together they made biscuits and microwavable bookmarks.

[52] Unsupported mammary glands often seen near garden centres.

[53] Generic term for most practising osteopaths.

[54] Any biological father of a chaise longue.

[55] The bits that stick out when you feel a drowsy numbness under your dimmocks.

[56] An area of the body most bishops want repositioned.

[57] The ultra sensitive danglers behind your Finsbury flinchers and above your Crouchenders.

Jack   That's it! The Shepherds Gonzalez *('Ah-Ah-Ah-Ah'. The* **Dame** *freezes. Remembering.*) You will find the answer in the sky. The beanstalk! I have to climb the beanstalk! I don't know why and I don't know what I'll find up (*Looking at the pot plant, confused.*) . . . there, but I have to go! Mum? Mum! (*The* **Dame** *unfreezes.*) I must get supplies: ladder, rope, Tupperware harness, helmet, torch . . . (*And he's gone, not even a goodbye.*)

Dame (*calling after him*)   Jack . . . Jack.

SONG SEVEN: MY BOY

When I felt him kick inside me
I knew just who he would be
So strong and with adventure
So desperate to be free

Then he was only fragile
And I held him in my arms
And he looked at me with such big eyes
Turning on the charms

Yes he's my boy
Shield him from the light
Yes he's my boy in the morning
But he'll be someone's man tonight

When it snowed I shouted gloves, dear
In the sun, you wear your cap
He just smiled at me and did it
When I left him he looked back

But he grew so fast and steady
Did things that seemed absurd
When I tried to ask him what was wrong
He wouldn't say a word

He was my boy
Shield him from the light
He was my boy in the morning
But he'll be someone's man tonight

A mum prepares her young to leave the nest one day
But then when that day comes it's like a piece of you can't
stay

He's was my boy
Shield him from the light
He was my boy in the morning-time
But he'll be someone's man tonight

Scene Three

The Woods near the Border

Narrator   The woods near the border of Nowen. Grimm enters with a crazy evil detector, her prized evil-o-meter. It's basically a contraption in the shape of a large pole with a . . .

Grimm (*out of character*)   Yep, got it!

Narrator (*out of character*)   Nobody tells me anything Michael! (*Or real name of actor, exits.*)

Grimm *walks around with her Tupperware-based contraption beeping and flashing as it detects different levels of good and evil in the vicinity. It seems to be on the blink.*

Grimm   Come on, come on, you stupid machine! Time is running out. (*She hits it.*) Only one more day before the wedding! If I don't find her soon then all my plans for world domination will be scuppered. (*She hits it again, this time it jolts into action.*) That's better. Blurgh, there's an awful lot of good in here . . . (*To someone in the audience.*) Not so much here, though. What have you been up to . . . naughty! (*Continuing around the audience.*) Eurgh, more good, disgusting! (*The machine starts to go out of control.*) Huh? What's going on? No, no . . . (*The contraption breaks down.*) Oh great! You've gone and broken my evil-o-meter by being so . . . good!

A figure appears from a puff of smoke.

Shepherd Dave   I am a Shepherd Gonzalez! (*Quickly.*) Ah-Ah-Ah-Ah. What can I do for you?

Grimm   What?

Shepherd Dave   I am a Shepherd Gonzalez! (*Quickly.*) Ah-Ah-Ah-Ah. What can I do for you?

Grimm   Nothing, plobslopper.[58]

Shepherd Dave   Plobslopper? That's a bit harsh. I was only asking if you wanted any help.

Grimm   Why would I want any help from you, you plidbibbler![59]

Shepherd Dave   Plidbibbler now! Unbelieveable! (*To self, closing eyes.*) Breath Dave, just breath. (*Inhales deeply a couple of times.*) In with the white light, out with the black smoke. It's my job. I'm an oracle. We do random acts of kindness that sort of thing.

Grimm   Ooh, how disgusting! No thanks.

Shepherd Dave   Sure? We can do anything.

Grimm   Really? Then fix this.

Shepherd Dave   No problem. (*Examining it.*) Ah yes, it just needs a new piddle sprocket.[60] Got one in the shed. (*Exits.*)

Shepherd Kofi *enters.*

Grimm   That was quick.

Shepherd Kofi   What was quick?

Grimm   Getting my piddle sprocket.

Shepherd Kofi   What piddle sprocket?

Grimm (*signalling her contraption*)   The piddle sprocket I need!

Shepherd Kofi   Oh. That must have been Dave.

Grimm   Dave?

---

[58] A pre-emptive and post-watershed insult.
[59] A shed made out of water.
[60] A four-dimensional menswear department.

Shepherd Kofi   I'll go get him.

Shepherd Kofi *exits,* **Shepherds Gary** *and* **Boutros** *enter.*

Grimm   So?

Shepherd Gary   So what?

Grimm   Where is it?

Shepherd Boutros   Where's what?

Grimm   Are you *total* idiots?

Shepherd Gary   Possibly.

Grimm   You lot are useless. I'll fix it myself.

Grimm *exits.* **Shepherds Kofi** *and* **Dave** *enter.*

Shepherd Boutros   Ooh, hark at her! 'I'll fix it myself'.

Shepherd Dave   Piece of work, that one.

Shepherd Kofi   Not half!

Shepherd Boutros   Don't you just love Oracle Directive three seven four part c.

Shepherd Dave   Ah, that's my favourite Oracle Directive!

All Shepherds   'Oracles do not and must not help bad people. Ever.'

Shepherd Gary   She really upset me though!

Shepherd Kofi   Don't worry, Gary, she'll see the error of her ways.

Shepherd Gary   Will she?

They all look out in thought, perusing the future. They see something – her future – and, in unison, turn to each other, happy and nodding.

All Shepherds (*smiling*)   Yep!

Shepherd Kofi (*to* **Shepherd Gary**)   But I see you are still troubled, my incredibly handsome shepherd friend. Perhaps a rustic love ballad would calm the turbulence in your soul?

Shepherd Gary   I think it would, yes.

Shepherd Kofi (*nodding to the others*)   The Cara Mison.[61]

The **Shepherds** *solemnly prepare their invisible instruments. This is gonna be a weepy one. One produces some tissues and hands a few out to the other members and the audience.*

Shepherd Boutros   'Tis but a simple tale of love, betrayal and the redemptive power of Tupperware.

Shepherd Gary   Yes, that's exactly the type of rustic love ballad I need to hear right now, Boutros.

Shepherd Boutros   Take it away, Dave!

During the song we see a passionate dance routine by the **Shepherds** *brandishing two pieces of Tupperware. At first at they are apart and then become united – a matching pair.*

SONG EIGHT: CARA MISON

[**Shepherd Dave**]   Somekepeo-masetto
Koromose-endason Queboa
Koromose-mepete-olandrento
Koromoso-jahando
Koromose-mepete-olontana
Koromose-hendene-hendene-koloso

[**All Shepherds**]   Cara Mison
CarA mos'onca polente
CarA mi sopa mere syia
Que topo de raya
Quesa de mison

Cara Mison
CarA mos'onca polente
CarA mi sopa mere syia
Que topo de raya
Quesa de mison

---

[61] The Cara Mison – Constructed by the partially partial following 'The Burning of the Tupperware' in the late Eight Shen under the supposed tutelage of Nibby Nibson.

[Shepherd Dave]   Entrove-amo banzana
    Suki-monseseba ledo
    Suki-monsese-monsese-monsese banzana
    Suki-moleleo baa
    Qwueneth-o-qwueneth- o-qwueneth bambolaba
    Qwueneth-umbaba-umbabah-jo

[All Shepherds]   Cara Mison
    CarA mos'onca polente
    CarA mi sopa mere syia
    Que topo de raya
    Quesa de mison

    Cara Mison
    CarA mos'onca polente
    CarA mi sopa mere syia
    Que topo de raya
    Quesa de mison

Shepherd Gary   That was wonderful. My former strife is but a distant shadow.

Shepherd Ban Ki   It's so nice to see Tupperware reunited. It's such a cause for celebration.

Shepherd Kofi   And there are others here tonight who have good cause to celebrate.

Shepherd Dave   Now being oracles we're all psychic but Kofi here has a very special skill. He can channel your energies into his head and . . . channel, channel, channel . . . down onto . . . his bottom.

Shepherd Boutros   It's true – all sorts of wise words and prophecies have appeared on his bum!

Shepherd Gary   Okay, how are you feeling, Kofi?

Shepherd Dave (*whipping the audience up into a frenzy*)   Everybody. Bottom, bottom, bottom . . . (*Etc.*)

Shepherd Kofi *clenches his buttocks and focuses hard. The chanting reaches its peak and* **Shepherd Boutros** *pulls down his trousers from behind.* **Shepherd Boutros** *then reads the* *announcements of* **Shepherd Kofi**'s *bottom. This process is repeated as many times as necessary in order to get through all the announcements. In reality the card with the names can be attached to the back of his boxer shorts before this scene.*

Shepherd Kofi   So for everyone who's celebrating their special day, let's sing Happy Birthday . . . in ancient Nowenthian!

The **Shepherds** *teach the audience the ancient Nowenthian version of Happy Birthday, including the compulsory gestures. Perhaps one of the actor carries on a board with the words.*

Shepherd Dave   Right, let's sing it through for them once.

SONG SHEET

[All Shepherds]   Kempe sembe pu te[62]
  Kempe sembe pu te
  Kempe loro se masu

Shepherd Kofi   Now the more astute will have realised that this third line is in fact slightly different. Can anyone tell me why? That's right, it's the subjunctive non-reflective future and past tense meaning may all your birthdays be filled with joy and your elbows never buckle.

[All Shepherds]   Kempe sembe pu te

Shepherd Kofi   Fantastic. Now let's all try together. Ready?

The song is performed three times, getting progressively faster – and ending in verbal chaos.

Scene Four

Jack's Farmhouse in Nowen

Narrator   Yet more crops are dying and with no dairy animals, everyone is starving. Seeing the giant, rotting

---

[62] The origins of the Kempe Sembe are unknown although curiously all races in the land of Waa claim ownership. Most marriages end and all wars start with a discussion about who it belongs to. If they all knew the correct translation of it, they really wouldn't bother.

beanstalk on their farm, the villagers believe that Jack and Tina are responsible for the curse that has descended on them. Angry, they start to gather in protest outside Jack and Tina's house.

The **Dame** *is sitting studying a piece of Tupperware with a special magnifying glass. A knock at the door.*

Dame   I'm, uh . . . not in!

Another knock.

Grimm   Hello?

And another.

Dame   If you're from the village, go away. It's not our fault.

Grimm   No, I'm not from these parts. I'm looking for my daughter. She ran away.

The **Dame** *opens the door.*

Dame   Oh you poor thing, do come in.

Grimm   Thank you. I'm just worried she'll do something awful to herself. You know how young people are. (*The* **Dame** *nods.*) She fell in with the wrong crowd, got mixed up in all kinds of things and (*Privately.*) I think she's started using yam-yam-quod.[63]

Dame   Yam-yam- quod! Oh dear. My Uncle Janet's daughter got hooked on that. A terrible business. I'm sorry, I haven't seen her.

Grimm   (*aside*) Strange, the beanstalk is here, she *must* be near. (*To the* **Dame**.) I have to find her.

Dame   And find her we will. But first let me get you a cucuppski of something to calm your nerves? Steaming Niflwuang,[64] Jasmin Tobbs[65] or perhaps a Herbal Bishop?

---

[63] A highly addictive rectangular shaped vegetable that leads to prolonged bouts of happiness followed by world peace – currently banned, contraband and Edmilliband.
[64] The best drink known to anyone ever.
[65] Any beverage not containing Jasmine.

Grimm   I'd love a Herbal Bishop! Thank you.

Dame   Skinny?

Grimm   Normal.

Dame   De-Klapth?[66]

Grimm   Full.

Dame   Eddie?

Grimm   Stobart. (*Beat.*) I'm watching the weight.

Dame   Just be a moment.

The **Dame** *exits.* **Grimm** *looks around, intrigued by the Tupperware collection. She puts her hand to her chest. For the first time we see she also has a necklace. Could it possibly be the matching piece?*

Jack (*bursting in*)   Mum! (*Sees* **Grimm**.) Mum?!

Grimm   I'm looking for my daughter. She's about your age. Have you seen her?

Jack   Sorry, no. Where's my mum?

Grimm   She'll be back in a minute. In a hurry?

Jack   Yes. Can you tell her I'm heading up to the top of that. (*He attempts to point to the window.*)

Grimm   What, the table?

Jack   Oh sorry, that! (*He points downwards.*)

Grimm   The floor?

Jack   I've never been very good at pointing.

Grimm   How are you with nodding?

Jack   Er, my nodding's not bad actually. I mean, I'm no expert . . .

Grimm   Alright, give me your best nod.

---

[66] A rash-inducing moral stance.

Jack *nods 'No'*.

Grimm   Why don't you want to nod?

Jack   I do. I did. But I nodded 'no' when I meant to nod 'yes'.

Grimm   Your nodding's not that much better than your pointing to be honest, is it?

Jack   No, sorry. Look, can you just tell her Jack's gone up the beanstalk.

Grimm   Up the beanstalk?

Jack   Yes, the answer is in the sky!

Grimm (*aside*)   Excellent. You'll be the first meal for my giant. (*Consulting her Tupperware watch.*) He'll just be waking up.

Jack   Sorry, what?

Grimm   Run along.

Jack (*exiting*)   Okay, bye nice lady!

Grimm   Imbecile!

She continues to look around the room, admiring the Tupperware. The **Dame** *re-enters with two mugs.*

Grimm (*noticing a particular piece*)   My word, is that an early Party Susan? Seventh Sheng[67] if I'm not mistaken.

Dame   Sixth, actually.

The **Dame** *picks it up.*

Grimm   Pre flom-fosb?

Dame   Pre flom-fosb.

Grimm   Do you mind if I . . .

Dame (*passing it to* **Grimm**)   Be my guest.

Grimm *takes it from her.*

---

[67] The epoch stretching from the Big Bang to the Little Plop, often available in Lycra.

Grimm   I love Tupperware.

Dame   How rare to find someone with the same passion.

Grimm   There's something I'd really like to show you.

Dame   I was going to say the same thing to you!

*They both take out their respective Tupperware necklaces (we have not fully seen **Grimm**'s before) and place them together. They are a pair! We hear the 'Sister, sister' sound effect.*

Dame (*awe struck*)   They fit!

Grimm   I can't believe it.

Dame   Georgina?

Grimm   Tina?

EastEnders – end of episode drums . . . Lights dip then back up.

Grimm   I thought you were . . .

Dame   I didn't know what happened.

Grimm   What do you remember?

Dame   I remember playing hide and seek with you. And then suddenly out of nowhere a massive five footed Grungol-Best[68] galloped in and took me away.

Grimm   The footprints! I assumed it was giants.

Dame   No, it was the Grungol-Best.

Grimm   How did you escape?

Dame   Well, it's quite a story . . .

EastEnders – end of episode drums . . . Lights dip then back up.

Grimm   Wow, you're right, that *was* quite a story.

Dame   And that's when we decided to buy a drum kit.

We expect the EastEnders tune again – perhaps not this time!

---

[68] A seven footed, eight toed and nine tongued version of the same.

Grimm Oh dear. I've made a terrible mistake.

Dame What is it?

Grimm (*panicking*) I daren't even tell you.

Dame You must.

Grimm (*starting to hyperventilate*) What have I done!

Dame Just tell me!

Grimm (*her breathing getting worse*) I can't . . . I . . .

Dame Oh darling, you're my blood. I won't judge you, no matter what you say!

Grimm (*the arrow through her heart*) Argh!

Dame Oh dear, let me get something to settle your nerves. (*She reaches for a Tupperware jar.*) Here, have some yam-yam-quod. (*Aside.*) Needs must! (*To* **Grimm**.) This'll calm you down for a while.

Grimm No, no . . . no! (*Too late, she has swallowed the yam-yam-quod. Slurring her words.*) But we need to tell your son . . .

Dame Yes, we need to tell Jack you're here, love!

Grimm (*the words now too hard to pronounce*) He's gone up the . . .

Dame What's that?

Grimm (*now very unintelligible*) He's gone up the . . . .

Dame . . . Oh you can't wait to meet your nephew, can you!

Grimm (*totally unintelligible*) He's gone up the . . . . (*Beat. Much clearer, but the yam-yam-quod has now set in.*) You've got six ears!

Dame Let's get you some air!

They exit. A moment. A knock at the door. Nothing. Again.

Inspector (*offstage*)   Hello? Anyone there? Ms Tina? Ms Tina? It's Inspector Thrushp. We have an order to uproot your beanstalk. It's sucking up all the nutrients from the land and destroying everything around it. I'm sorry about the lack of warning but there's nothing we can do. It's beyond my jurisdiction. (*The door opens.* **Inspector Thrushp** *enters.*) Ms Tina? (*Shouting offstage.*) There's nobody here. Okay, let's get started.

Inspector *exits. Shouting off and the sound of diggers pulling up and men with axes and ropes etc.*

Scene Five

The Top of the Beanstalk

Narrator   The top of the beanstalk . . . (*Turns the page, expecting more.*) Nope, that's it. The top of the beanstalk. (*Realises.*) Ooh, it's the fight scene!

Through the smoke, the beastly figure of **Geoff** *can be made out. His eyes are closed. His body is wet and glistening. Giant bean stems that trail off into the wings are attached to his chest, arms, legs and mouth. At first his eyes are closed. We hear his deep breathing.*

Jack *approaches, sees* **Geoff** *and freezes. When he realises he's not awake he creeps around him, looking with intrigue, his heart beating fast.*

Geoff *begins to wake . . . He opens his eyes. He doesn't know where or what he is, only that he is pure evil. He spits the bean stem out of his mouth and splutters.* **Jack** *hides. Then with an almighty roar* **Geoff** *casts off the remaining stems.*

Geoff (*sniffing*)   Fee. Fi. Fo. Fum. I smell the blood of a Nowenthian.

Jack *sneaks a peek, but* **Geoff** *turns towards him and he retracts.*

Geoff (*sniffing*)   Be him alive or be him dead, I'll grind his bones to make my bread.

Jack *emerges.*

Jack Here I am, you beast! I shall slay thee with mine axe.

Geoff A pox on your axe. My Gazoobian ball and chain shall crusheth thee.

Jack (*realising they don't have the props he breaks character*) Shall we use the rapiers from Hamlet?

Geoff (*out of character*) Where are they?

Jack (*out of character, pointing to the top corner of the theatre*) There!

Geoff (*out of character*) On the roof?

Jack (*out of character*) Sorry, I've got pointing issues. There! (*points to his face*)

Geoff (*out of character*) In your nose?

Jack (*out of character, going to fetch them*) Here.

Geoff (*out of character*) Thanks.

Jack *retrieves the rapiers and passes one to* **Geoff**. *He changes his mind and swaps them over. He repeats this until* **Geoff** *has had enough.*

Geoff (*out of character*) Omar! (*Or real name of actor.*)

Jack (*out of character*) There's only one way to settle this!

Geoff (*out of character*) A quick round of Japperson Queg?

Jack (*out of character, with audience*) Japperson!

Geoff (*out of character*) Queg.

Jack (*out of character, with audience*) Japperson!

Geoff (*out of character*) Queg.

Jack (*out of character, with audience*) Japperson! (*Etc.*)

They start to duel – it's serious Shakespearean actor time again.

Jack (**Hamlet**) (**Jack** *nips the* **Geoff** *on the arm*) A hit, a very palpable hit.

They continue duelling, this time **Geoff** *nips* **Jack** *on the arm.*

Geoff (**Laertes**)   Have at you!

They continue duelling, **Geoff** *nips* **Jack** *on the arm again.*

Geoff (**Laertes**)   Another hit. What say you?

Jack (**Hamlet**)   A touch, a touch. I do confess'd. (*Breaking character.*) You're actually pretty tiny for a giant, aren't you?

Geoff   No, I'm not.

Jack   Yeah, you are, you're way smaller than me.

Geoff   Oh, small am I?

Geoff *lunges at* **Jack** *and roars.* **Jack** *stumbles back and drops his rapier. Quick as a flash* **Geoff** *grabs it and holds both rapier points to* **Jack**'s *throat.*

Geoff   What have you got to say for yourself now, heh?

Jack   Would 'I'm sorry' help?

Geoff   Of course not. Time to say goodbye!

He draws back the swords and is about to pounce when . . .

Grenthel   No! Stop this.

Jack   I agree.

Geoff   Who are you to intrude, you pathetic little pemsplat?[69]

Grenthel   I've come for you, Geoff. I promised I would.

Geoff   What are you talking about?

Grenthel   It's me, Grenthel. Don't you remember? (**Geoff** *is confused.*) My mother miniaturised you into a bean so you would grow evil and help her take over the world.

Jack   The beans!

---

[69] In of itself not very much – but why not.

Grenthel   Geoff, you're a good giant, you're a gentle giant, you're a . . .

Geoff   Nonsense. I'm an evil giant! Time to eat you!

Grenthel *produces the locket.*

Grenthel   Wait. Remember this locket that you didn't give to me because we couldn't find it in Act One?

Geoff   Yes. (**Geoff** *looks for the first time like there's something familiar.*)   But I'm evil!

Grenthel   Oh my fair Geoff. Where be your jibes now, your gambols, your songs, your flashes of merriment that will want to set the table on a roar. (*Gestures to the audience member to pass on Yorrick's skull.*) Alas, poor Geoff, I knew him well.

Geoff   I'm not dead, sweetheart – but you're about to be! (*He lunges towards them but is torn between good and evil.*)   No, I must eat you . . . I want to . . . But I can't . . . Must eat . . . (*To the audience.*) Should I eat them?

The audience interact. Even after this he decides to eat them. He roars a huge roar.

Geoff   No! I am evil and I will be satisfied!

He charges towards **Jack** *and is about to kill him when* **Grenthel** *points to her ears and makes the silent sound which stops him in his tracks. He puts his hands to his head in pain for a few moments but he is more powerful now and can endure it.*

Grenthel (*to the audience*)   Please help me, everyone. We need to do this together to expel the evil powers in Geoff. Remember this (*She makes the silent sound.*), the silent sound that all giants hate? Point to your ears and make the silent sound with me. After three, one two three!

Once again this stops **Geoff** *in his tracks and he is in obvious pain.* **Grenthel** *encourages the audience 'Make more silent noise!' etc. But* **Geoff** *is fighting back.*

Grenthel   Jack, we need you too.

Jack   But, but I can't point! I'm useless at pointing.

Grenthel   Face your fear, Jack. You can point and you will point. Point, Jack. You can do it. Can't he everyone?

With a concerted effort and the encouragement of the audience, **Jack** *points in his ears and makes the silent sound with* **Grenthel** *and the audience. Finally, all the evil is driven out of* **Geoff**, *who lies exhausted on the floor.*

REPRISE: WHEREVER YOU GO

[**Grenthel**]   Remember Grimm my mother who is evil
   At the workhouse behind the iron gate
   We planned to run away one night together
   But she trapped you in a bean inside a crate

   I'll always find you
   Wherever you go
   Even if you change your name to . . .

Geoff   Wait!

Grenthel   Yes?

[**Geoff**]   I've beaned through valleys, of wheat and barley
   I'm sorry but I changed my name to Boutros Boutros-
   Ghali

Grenthel   That's okay.
   Yes you have found me and you have freed my heart

[**Both**]   A life without you here
   I can't abide.

Grenthel   You see, you're not evil at all.

Jack   Are you sure? He did just try to eat us!

Grenthel   It's all over now. He's a gentle giant.

Jack   You keep saying giant, but he's the same size as us.

Grenthel   I know. Back home they call him the smallest giant in the world. And I love him!

Geoff Grenthel?

Grenthel I promised I'd find you.

*The actor playing **Geoff** turns away and applies a spray of breath freshener into his mouth.*

They kiss.

Geoff Wow! Kissing's much better than fighting – no matter what religion you are!

Grenthel Come on, Geoff, let's get down this beanstalk.

Jack What about your family? Are they all tiny too?

Geoff I'm not *tiny*! I don't have a family.

Jack Not even a mum!

Geoff No.

Jack You should come and meet my mum. She's mum enough for both of us!

Geoff Are you going to adopt me? That's brilliant!

Jack (*back-peddling*) Oh, I'm, uh, not saying we're going to adopt you, I'm just saying she's lovely.

They exit in deep discussion about what was and what was not said.

Scene Six

Jack's Farmhouse in Nowen

Shepherd Gary All's well that ends well – and our work here is nearly done. That means that very soon you'll be back in the comfort of your own home, sitting on the sofa with a cucuppski of Herbal Bishop, emailing all your friends and spreading the word about the Shepherds Gonzalez through Twitter and Facebook. Oh yes, we may be based in Waa but we understand your curious ways.

*The **Dame** and **Grimm** enter, holding each other. The effects of
yam-yam-quod have not entirely worn off **Grimm**.*

Grimm   And that's how Auntie Brian got his false feet.

Sounds of digging machinery, ripping of the land etc.

Grimm (*rushing to the window*)   What's that?

Dame   Oh, no. The villagers.

Grimm   What are they doing?

Dame   They're ripping up the beanstalk. (*Shouting out of the
window.*) No! Wait! Oh where's Jack?

Grimm (*remembering*)   That's what I was trying to tell you.
I'm so sorry, Tina. Jack went up the . . .

Jack, Grenthel *and* **Geoff** *enter.*

Jack (*to* **Grenthel** *and* **Geoff** *as he enters*)   . . . massive
beanstalk! (*To the* **Dame.**) Mother, this is . . .

Grenthel (*seeing* **Grimm**)   . . . Mother?

Jack   Yes. This is my mother.

Grenthel   And this is *my* mother.

Coronation Street theme tune plays . . .

Dame   Jack, you're safe!

Geoff   Ms Grimm! What's going on?

Grimm   Please call me Georgina.

Grenthel   What are you doing here? Can't you leave
us alone?

Grimm   Grenthel, I'm so so sorry.

Geoff   The lady doth protest too much.

Grimm   I'm just so happy you're alive and well.

Grenthel   I find that hard to believe!

Dame Georgina?

Grimm Yes, she's right. I've been so cruel all these years. I'm sorry, Geoff – and Grenthel, I don't want you to marry the Prince of Senpebs.

Geoff You don't?

Jack Mum, what's going on?

Dame Georgina is my sister.

Jack Auntie? (*He goes and hugs her.*) Auntie!

Grimm Tina?

Dame I suppose we're all allowed to turn over a new leaf – no matter what religion we are.

Jack In case you didn't understand that, let's do it again . . . in multiple languages.

The actors replay the scene from **Grenthel**'*s line 'Mother?' to the* **Dame**'*s line 'I suppose we're all allowed to turn over a new leaf – no matter what religion we are' each actor taking on a different language (suggestions: Spanish/Danish/Mandarin/Urdu/sign language).*

Geoff And gosh, what a relief that we can all be so mature about the whole thing and forgive each other instantly. That's the redemptive power of Tupperware for you. Who loves Tupperware?

Audience interact.

A moo.

Jack It can't be.

Another moo.

Jack I'd recognise that moo anywhere!

A bark.

Jack It's . . . (*Thrown by the bark.*) it's Daisy!

Dame   Where?

With a cast of five, the actors use a backup fury animal toy to play **Daisy**.

Jack   Here. (*As* **Daisy**.) Hello! (*As* **Jack**.) Daisy! You can talk? (*As* **Daisy**.) Oh, yes. I had the most amazing time with the Shepherds Gonzalez. I've become their manager. Their music's great but they completely lack any sense of business acumen. I'm quite the dab hand at band management apparently. And it turns out Inspector Thrushp is a massive fan. (*As* **Jack**.) Really? (*As* **Daisy**.) Yes, he's made an exception and given me a permit to tour with them. Tour starts next week. But I said no. (*As* **Jack**.) You said no? (*As* **Daisy**.) I said not until I've asked my best friend Jack. (*As* **Jack**.) Oh Daisy, I'm delighted for you. Of course you can go. (*As* **Daisy**.) Thank you Jack. (*As* **Jack**.) Thank you, Daisy, for being the bestest friend anyone could dream of.

They hug.

Grimm   Thank you, Tina, for never losing faith in me.

Dame   Thank you, Georgina, for making me and our Rhombus Podge finally complete.

They join the Rhombus Podge together one more time and hug.

Geoff   Thank you, Grenthel, for saving my life and introducing me to the wonderful world of kissing.

Grenthel   Thank you, Geoff, for being the bestest, bravest and smallest giant in the world.

An ethereal 'Ah-Ah-Ah-Ah in the distance'. The **Dame**, **Jack**, **Grenthel**, **Geoff** *and* **Grimm** *look up to the sky* . . .

Shepherd Ban Ki (*V/O*)   Thank you, Gary, for believing in me.

Shepherd Gary (*V/O*)   Thank you, Dave, for showing me how Tupperware can change lives.

Shepherd Kofi (*V/O*)   Thank you, Boutros, for always being there to read names that appear on my bottom.

Shepherd Dave (*V/O*)   Thank you, Kofi, for letting me sleep on your sofa. I promise, just a few more days.

Shepherd Boutros (*V/O*)   Thank you all for another successful mission.

The sound of the Shepherd's mothership moving away . . .

All (*waving to the sky*)   And thank you, Shepherds Gonzalez.

Geoff *puckers up his lips hoping for another kiss.* **Grenthel** *kisses him.*

Dame   You see, it doesn't matter if you're tall, small or absolutely medium. It's what's on the inside that counts.

They all turn out to the audience.

All   No matter what religion you are!

Geoff   I want to shout out thank you to all these lovely boys and girls. Because without them, there would have been no Jack and the Beanstalk. Without them, I would be evil not gentle and more importantly without them, we'd still have three more acts of Hamlet to do.

Jack   If anyone does want to see my Hamlet, I'm going to do a one-man show entitled . . .

Dame (*out of character*)   . . . yes, yes thank you Omar! (*Or real name of actor.*)

SONG NINE: FEE FI FO FUM [REPRISE]

Up where the clouds lie
Along the hillside
Here where the sun shines on the crops all day
We climb and gather
Working together
And so we sing this
As we work away

And yes we say [x3]
Hey-o Hey-o where the crops grow
Hi-di-hey-di-o Hey-o Hey-o
Fee Fi Fee Fi Fo Fum – Fee Fi Fo Fum

We'll toil the land and
We lend a hand and
We work together as a giant team
We pick the finest
We wash and dry best
We sort and sample
Then we pack the beans

And yes we say [x3]
Hey-o Hey-o where the crops grow
Hi-di-hey-di-o Hey-o Hey-o
Fee Fi Fee Fi Fo Fum – Fee Fi Fo Fum

Shepherd Kofi   And so it was that Georgina Grimm inadvertently brought the trading of beans to Nowen. The workhouse back in Gazoob was disbanded and all the gentle giants lived happily on the farm with Jack, Tina, Georgina, Geoff, Grenthel and Daisy. The Shepherds Gonzalez's second album, entitled 'Introducing the Shepherds Gonzalez' went triple platinum but they continued to work as oracles in the wonderful land of Waa.

And yes we say [x3]
Hey-o Hey-o where the crops grow
Hi-di-hey-di-o Hey-o Hey-o
Fee Fi Fee Fi Fo Fum – Fee Fi Fo Fum

Jack (Hamlet)   The rest is silence.

Blackout.

BOWS

INSTRUMENTAL MEDLEY INTO . . .

Announcement (*V/O*)   Some of you know them as the
Santos Twins,[70] some as the Bosh Bosh Triplets[71] and others
as the Gazoobian mixed darts quartet. Ladies and
gentlemen, boys and girls, for one night only, I give you . . .
The Shepherds Gonzalez!

SONG TEN: SHEPHERD MEDLEY [REPRISE]

We are the Shepherds Gonzalez
We are Shepherds Gonzalez
We are the Shepherds Gonzalez
And we have a song for you

Whether you're a Christian, Muslim or Jew
Come and pull up a pew
Rastafarian, Buddhist or Sikh
Would you kindly take your seat

We are the Shepherds Gonzalez
We are Shepherds Gonzalez
We are the Shepherds Gonzalez
And we have a song for you

Shepherd Boutros   Boys and girls, ladies and gentlemen,
we hope you've enjoyed the show. Merry Christmas / Happy
New Year to one and all!

Doesn't matter what's buggin'
If you need a little lovin'
When you want a little huggin'
Just call out our name

Doesn't matter if you're teary
If you're feeling rather weary
When life is cold and dreary
Just call out our name

---

[70] Three halves of the recently defunct jazz infusion solo act 'Pencilectomy'.
[71] Experimental free form artichokes.

We are the Shepherds Gonzalez
The Shepherd Gonza-le-e-e-e-ez
We are the Shepherds Gonzalez
The Shepherd Gonza-le-ez

We are the Shepherd Gonza-a-a-a-a-a-a-a
le-e-e-e-e-e-e-ez
We're your Oracles
Just call out our name

We are the Shepherds Gonzalez
The Shepherd Gonza-le-e-e-e-ez
We are the Shepherds Gonzalez
The Shepherd Gonza-le-ez
We are the Shepherd Gonza-a-a-a-a-a-a-a
le-e-e-e-e-e-e-ez
We're your Oracles
Just call out our name

The **Shepherds Gonzalez** *lead the audience out of the auditorium in a conga.*

Score

Cara Mison

Song 8: (Act2, Sc3)

Music and Lyrics by Jez Bond
Arranged by Dimitri Scarlato

Rhumba   Cara Mison

Cara Mison

Vox. 1: Ca - ra Mi - son   Ca - ra mo-s'on-ca   po - len-te
Vox. 2: Ca - ra Mi - son   Ca - ra mo-s'on-ca   po - len-te
Vox. 3: Ca - ra Mi - son   Ca - ra mo-s'on-ca   po - len-te
Vox. 4: Ca - ra Mi - son   Ca - ra mo-s'on-ca   po - len-te
Pno.: Emin   Amin

Vox. 1: Ca-ra mi so-pa me-re sy-ia Que to-po de ra - ya   Que-sa de mi - son
Vox. 2: Ca-ra mi so-pa me-re sy-ia Que to-po de ra - ya   Que-sa de mi - son
Vox. 3: Ca-ra mi so-pa me-re sy-ia Que to-po de ra - ya   Que-sa de mi - son
Vox. 4: Ca-ra mi so-pa me-re sy-ia Que to-po de ra - ya   Que-sa de mi - son
Pno.: Cmaj7   B   Emin

Score

Fee Fi Fo Fum

Song 1: (Act1, Sc1)

Music & Lyrics by Jez Bond
Arrangement by Dimitri Scarlato

Here in the moun - tains   Be-hind the iron gates   There lies a work house for

gen - tle giants   No-bo-dy loves us   In-side the work-house   No-bo-dy

Vox. 1: ah Fee fi fee fi fo fum fee fi fo fum

Vox. 2: ah Fee fi fee fi fo fum fee fi fo fum

Grimm Spoken: Hmm, this new hair straightener needs work. Ah, ah , ah! I'll reset the dobby and tighten up the squelding belt

Vox. 3: ah Fee fi fee fi fo fum fee fi fo fum

Vox. 2: We toil the land and we lend a hand and

Vox. 3: We toil the land and we lend a hand and

Score

Fee Fi Fo Fum

Reprise Song 1: (Act1, Sc1)

Music & Lyrics by Jez Bond
Arranged by Dimitri Scarlato

©

Fee Fi Fo Fum

Score

I'll Always Find You

Song 4: (Act1, Sc6)

Music by Jez Bond
Lyrics by Jez Bond & Mark Cameron
Arranged by Dimitri Scarlato

©

I'll Always Find You

Score

If I Were

Song 3: (Act1, Sc5)

Music by Jez Bond
Lyrics by Jez Bond & Mark Cameron
Arranged by Dimitri Scarlato

so much of life__ that's left_ to see__ I've lost all my friends and fa __ mi - ly__ to

Bo - vine spon - gi-form en - ce - pha - lo - pa - thy_____

B S E _____ Yes it's clear to see

It's B S E _____ Don't blame me

If I Were

Continute scatting ad libitum until exit

Score

Just Call Out Our Name

Song 6: (Act2, Sc1)

Music & Lyrics by Jez Bond
Arrangement by Dimitri Scarlato

©

Just Call Out Our Name

Just Call Out Our Name

Score

My Boy

Song 7: (Act2, Sc7)

Music and Lyrics by Jez Bond
Arranged by Dimitri Scarlato

When I

felt him kick in-side me I knew just who he would be So strong and with ad-ven - ture So

des-per-ate to be free Then he was on - ly fra-gile And I held him on___ my arms And he

©

My Boy

Score

My Plan

Song 5: (Act1, Sc8)

Music & Lyrics by Jez Bond
Arrangement by Dimitri Scarlato

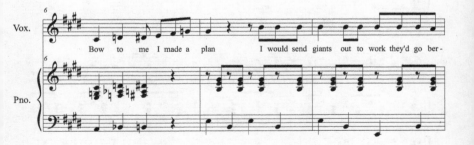

©

My Plan

My Plan

Score

We are the Shepherds

Song 2: (Act1, Sc4)

Music & Lyrics by Jez Bond and Mark Cameron
Arrangement by Dimitri Scarlato

We are the Shepherds

Vox. 1: We are the she-pherds Gon za lez and we're here to help you Whe-ther you're a

Vox. 2: We are the she-pherds Gon - za - lez and we're here to help you Whe-ther you're a

Vox. 3: we are the she-pherds Gon - za - lez and we're here to help you Whe-ther you're a

Vox. 1: Chri-stian Mu - slim or Jew Come and pull up — a pew Ra - sta -

Vox. 2: Chri-stian Mu - slim or Jew Come and pull up — a pew Ra - sta -

Vox. 3: Chri-stian Mu - slim or Jew Come and pull up — a pew Ra - sta -

fa - rian Bud - dhist or Sikh   Would you kind - ly take your seat

fa - rian Bud - dhist or Sikh   Would you kind - ly take your seat

fa - rian Bud - dhist or Sikh   Would you kind - ly take your seat

We are the she-pherds Gon - za - lez   We are the she-pherds Gon - za - lez

We are the she-pherds Gon - za - lez   We are the she-pherds Gon - za - lez

we are the she-pherds Gon - za - lez   we are the she-pherds Gon - za - lez

We are the Shepherds

We are the Shepherds

Bloomsbury Methuen Drama Modern Plays

include work by

Bola Agbaje
Edward Albee
Davey Anderson
Jean Anouilh
John Arden
Peter Barnes
Sebastian Barry
Alistair Beaton
Brendan Behan
Edward Bond
William Boyd
Bertolt Brecht
Howard Brenton
Amelia Bullmore
Anthony Burgess
Leo Butler
Jim Cartwright
Lolita Chakrabarti
Caryl Churchill
Lucinda Coxon
Curious Directive
Nick Darke
Shelagh Delaney
Ishy Din
Claire Dowie
David Edgar
David Eldridge
Dario Fo
Michael Frayn
John Godber
Paul Godfrey
James Graham
David Greig
John Guare
Mark Haddon
Peter Handke
David Harrower
Jonathan Harvey
Iain Heggie

Robert Holman
Caroline Horton
Terry Johnson
Sarah Kane
Barrie Keeffe
Doug Lucie
Anders Lustgarten
David Mamet
Patrick Marber
Martin McDonagh
Arthur Miller
D. C. Moore
Tom Murphy
Phyllis Nagy
Anthony Neilson
Peter Nichols
Joe Orton
Joe Penhall
Luigi Pirandello
Stephen Poliakoff
Lucy Prebble
Peter Quilter
Mark Ravenhill
Philip Ridley
Willy Russell
Jean-Paul Sartre
Sam Shepard
Martin Sherman
Wole Soyinka
Simon Stephens
Peter Straughan
Kate Tempest
Theatre Workshop
Judy Upton
Timberlake Wertenbaker
Roy Williams
Snoo Wilson
Frances Ya-Chu Cowhig
Benjamin Zephaniah

Bloomsbury Methuen Drama Student Editions

Jean Anouilh *Antigone* • John Arden *Serjeant Musgrave's Dance* •
Alan Ayckbourn *Confusions* • Aphra Behn *The Rover* • Edward
Bond *Lear* • *Saved* • Bertolt Brecht *The Caucasian Chalk Circle* •
Fear and Misery in the Third Reich • *The Good Person of Szechwan* •
Life of Galileo • *Mother Courage and Her Children* • *The Resistible
Rise of Arturo Ui* • *The Threepenny Opera* • Anton Chekhov *The
Cherry Orchard* • *The Seagull* • *Three Sisters* • *Uncle Vanya* • Caryl
Churchill *Serious Money* • *Top Girls* • Shelagh Delaney *A Taste of
Honey* • Euripides *Elektra* • *Medea* • Dario Fo *Accidental Death
of an Anarchist* • Michael Frayn *Copenhagen* • John Galsworthy
Strife • Nikolai Gogol *The Government Inspector* • Carlo Goldoni
A Servant to Two Masters • Lorraine Hansberry *A Raisin in the
Sun* • Robert Holman *Across Oka* • Henrik Ibsen *A Doll's House*
• *Ghosts* • *Hedda Gabler* • Sarah Kane *4.48 Psychosis* • *Blasted* •
Charlotte Keatley *My Mother Said I Never Should* • Bernard Kops
Dreams of Anne Frank • Federico García Lorca *Blood Wedding*
• *Doña Rosita the Spinster* (bilingual edition) • *The House of
Bernarda Alba* (bilingual edition) • *Yerma* (bilingual edition) •
David Mamet *Glengarry Glen Ross* • *Oleanna* • Patrick Marber
Closer • John Marston *The Malcontent* • Martin McDonagh *The
Lieutenant of Inishmore* • *The Lonesome West* • *The Beauty Queen
of Leenane* • Arthur Miller *All My Sons* • *The Crucible* • *A View
from the Bridge* • *Death of a Salesman* • *The Price* • *After the Fall* •
The Last Yankee • *A Memory of Two Mondays* • *Broken Glass* • Joe
Orton *Loot* • Joe Penhall *Blue/Orange* • Luigi Pirandello *Six
Characters in Search of an Author* • Lucy Prebble *Enron* • Mark
Ravenhill *Shopping and F***ing* • Willy Russell *Blood Brothers* •
Educating Rita • Sophocles *Antigone* • *Oedipus the King* • Wole
Soyinka *Death and the King's Horseman* • Shelagh Stephenson
The Memory of Water • August Strindberg *Miss Julie* • J. M.
Synge *The Playboy of the Western World* • Theatre Workshop
Oh What a Lovely War • Frank Wedekind *Spring Awakening* •
Timberlake Wertenbaker *Our Country's Good* • Arnold Wesker
The Merchant • Oscar Wilde *The Importance of Being Earnest*
• Tennessee Williams *A Streetcar Named Desire* • *The Glass
Menagerie* • *Cat on a Hot Tin Roof* • *Sweet Bird of Youth*

For a complete listing of Bloomsbury
Methuen Drama titles, visit:
www.bloomsbury.com/drama

Follow us on Twitter and keep up to date
with our news and publications
@MethuenDrama